# You & Him

Getting to
the Heart of Your
Relationship Potential

Dr Pam Spurr

# You & Him

Getting to

the Heart of Your

Relationship Potential

Thorsons

Thorsons
An Imprint of HarperCollins*Publishers*
77–85 Fulham Palace Road,
Hammersmith, London W6 8JB

The Thorsons website address is: www.thorsons.com

Published by Thorsons 2000

1 3 5 7 9 10 8 6 4 2

© Dr Pam Spurr

Dr Pam Spurr asserts the moral right to
be identified as the author of this work

A catalogue record for this book
is available from the British Library

ISBN 0 7225 4023 X

Printed and bound in Great Britain by
Omnia Books Limited, Glasgow

# Contents

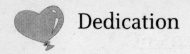 # Dedication

I dedicate this book to my husband, Nick, a wonderful man who helped me find the strength to stop needing 'too much, too soon'.

# Acknowledgements

I'd like to acknowledge that although this book has been written for women pursuing straight relationships, this in no way means that I'm ignoring the validity of relationships experienced by gays, lesbians, and bisexuals. However, I believe there are special issues pertaining to those that I could not have done justice to in this book. All should be fair in love and romance, and whatever the sexual orientation, people should have the freedom and confidence to pursue happy relationships.

I'd like to thank the numerous women, and men, who have spoken to me about their relationships with openness and honesty over the years. It's their stories that we can all learn from. It never ceases to amaze me how even the most guarded people will open up with time and patience. And how by far the majority place the central emphasis of their life on their intimate relationships. I'd like to acknowledge the tremendous encouragement I received from Wanda Whiteley and the sensitive editing of Caroline Brooke Johnson.

# Introduction

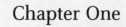

Chapter One

# Understanding The Relationship Puzzle

The Starting Point For Getting To The Heart
Of Your Relationship Potential!

Over the years, I've met many women who complain of a cycle
of unhappy relationships. I always begin by asking them about
their 'inner romantic dialogue'. This is the voice inside their
mind that goes over every single detail of the man they've just
met or recently been involved with. Details ranging from the
way he smiles ('Was that a cheeky smile or a smug smile?') to
second guessing what he's like in bed ('If he's a bit cheeky, he'll
probably be fun!'). It digests new romantic experiences ('I've
*never* had a man ring me the next day!'), mulls over the present

love interest, and compares him to past loves. It looks for good signs ('He doesn't remind me of my ex!') – and bad signs ('Uh-oh, he mentions his mother an awful lot!'). A running emotional narrative is provided. This inner dialogue is their barometer of romantic interest and fulfilment.

A common thread that seems to link these women is a stream of questions that their inner dialogue seems to wrestle with. I wonder, have *you* ever asked yourself any of the following questions:

1. 'Why do I feel this way about this man?'
2. 'Why do my relationships never fully succeed?'
3. 'Why doesn't he feel the way I do?'
   Or
4. 'Why doesn't he seem to give to the relationship what I give?'

If your answer is: 'Yes, I do ask myself these sorts of questions,' then this book is for *you* and *all women* who question the level of happiness their relationships bring.

Think about the first two questions. They apply to you and your essential self – the woman you bring to all your relationships. And the second two questions? They apply to why so many men seem to behave in mysterious ways when it comes to their romantic relationships. In fact, you may often feel you've entered an episode of *The X Files* when trying to fathom out the man in your life! The very fact that you, as a woman, even *ask* yourself these questions sets you apart from the average man you'll meet and become involved with. Men simply don't sit around, staring into their coffee cup, pondering the sorts of questions we do.

You won't catch them thinking about earth shattering dilemmas like: 'Her home's so untidy – I guess it's a sign she doesn't care about my feelings, so how am I going to make her care more?' And you won't catch them having conversations with their friends that consist of repeating the details of conversations they've had with you. All in the hopes of further understanding the relationship. The following just *won't* happen except in your imagination – your new man talking to a friend: 'When I said, "It *didn't* matter what she wore," then she got huffy because she said it *did* matter. But when I explained I didn't mean it *didn't* matter but that it didn't seem that important, then she got upset saying that *must* mean that I don't care if it doesn't seem important to me!'

Phew! Just writing up the sort of conversations women have amongst themselves, repeating everything they and their boyfriends said to one another is enough to understand why men don't go down that route! Such conversations are in a woman's quest to further her understanding of a relationship. But most men simply don't think about relationships in the way we do – even when their relationships are just as important. And that is why this book falls into two main parts. The first part will help you understand the person you are in terms of romantic relationships. And in putting the spotlight on your own feelings and behaviour, this will take you one half of the way to finding the sort of relationship you'd like. The second part of the book is about understanding the way men think, feel, and act in relationships, and where they believe sex and romance fit in. This is the second half of the equation. Put the two together and you can find and keep the relationship of your dreams. You can reach your relationship potential!

## 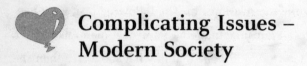 Complicating Issues – Modern Society

All the understanding in the world may still not be enough to find a worthy man and have a wonderful relationship. At a general level, there are all sorts of issues in modern society that put hurdles in the way of this very important pursuit. Let's take the most basic issue of the modern family – and what's happened to it. We no longer have those tight-knit, extended families keeping an eye open for suitable partners for us. Aunties and grannies, cousins and godparents are all wrapped up in the stress of modern living. They probably never even see much of you because you've long since moved away from the area of your birth. They wouldn't have a clue as to the sort of person to set you up with and quite frankly probably don't have the time to care.

This leaves you out in the cold fending for yourself. At your place of work, you keep a cautious eye on the other singles. Do any seem interested in you? Is it acceptable in terms of the office etiquette to make a move? Whenever you go to a social event, you try your hardest to look detached, and *not* desperate, even though you're scanning the scene for anyone who looks vaguely suitable and single. And, of course, you join those all-important clubs, evening classes, or sports centres. This in the hopes of finding a like-minded man who will at least meet the very basic requirement of having the social skills enabling participation in such a group!

##  Modern Courtship

But even if you end up with a single man in your sights what about the pitfalls of modern courtship? The boundaries have been blurred as to who makes what move. The modern dance of romance has all the grace of a near-sighted elephant lumbering about. You stumble towards each other with some vague notion that someone will open up a dialogue. You nervously flirt a bit and then wonder if you've given off the wrong message. Possibly you fall into bed straightaway, wanting to demonstrate your modern attitude and very often regret taking such action. Or you may even play the cool, confident woman role so well that men figure you're not interested! The problem lies in these behaviours not actually representing who you *are* and what your needs are, in terms of relationships. But rather whom you think you should try to be in the confused and muddy waters of modern romance! The very essence of *You & Him* is helping you understand you can reach your relationship potential once you understand more about the emotional forces that drive you in your relationships.

 # The Relationship Puzzle

So let's get more specific and think about your expectations when you approach a relationship. I'd like to introduce an essential concept here that I hope will shed some light on why at a fundamental level so many relationships fail. This is the concept of the 'relationship puzzle'. Think about the way you go through life, and the thought and effort you give to finding someone to share it with. With friends, you may discuss in detail their experiences of relationships. In fact 'men' may dominate your conversations. You look back over your past, picking through the twists and turns, and think over the things that didn't quite go the way you had planned. You think about your present situation and how you can find the right person. You get anxious over the future – that great, unknown romantic territory.

All this self-questioning about the rights and wrongs of things you've done, the wonder over how things could have been done differently, the sharing with friends, the ongoing self-analysis about the present and future is like putting together the pieces of a puzzle. Piece by piece you attempt, in the best way you can, to unlock the mystery and complete the overall relationship puzzle – by finding the man who you can have a happy relationship with.

## ♥ Trying To Find A Matching Puzzle Piece

The sticking point usually comes with the two most important pieces of that puzzle – you and him! What many women fail to recognize is that they look for a *match* to themselves – a puzzle piece, a man, who is their *equal* in an emotional sense, and in fact every sense. And in insisting a man match them, they attempt to bend and twist that man and try to force a fit between his puzzle piece and theirs. They try and change his little ways that irritate. They may try and get him to act differently or talk about his feelings more. Or they try and completely reshape his personality to one they think he *should* have or they'd be happy with him having!

This is where one of the most basic relationship problems starts: when one person feels they are not accepted for who they are and are under pressure to change. Of course, people do change as they mature and grow, or find themselves in new circumstances and in new relationships, and adapt to these in certain ways. They learn to compromise and to share. They develop knowledge about their new lover's boundaries. All this or their relationships are likely to fail. But this is quite different from being treated like a pliable piece of clay to be shaped as desired, as if you have no feelings or direction of your own. Understanding this difference will help you get to the heart of your relationship potential!

 ## Carol's Experience

I once saw a woman, Carol, who complained of a cycle of repeated failed relationships. When we looked closely at her past relationships, it became patently clear that every new man she met she tried to mould into someone like her father. He was doting and protective and in return Carol had always been an affectionate daughter who put him on a pedestal. She yearned to recreate that relationship with someone who'd adore her in the most demonstrative way – who she could then adore back and put on a pedestal.

No matter who the man was, no matter what his personality – distant or dependent – Carol tried to force him to behave to her as her father did. She would coax at first, dropping hints about the way she'd like to be treated. If coaxing didn't meet with enough success, she'd then go into her 'make-them-guess' mode. In this phase, they'd know something was wrong as she'd withdraw affection. But they'd have to keep guessing at what this 'wrong thing' was.

Sometimes they'd nearly make it through this phase. They'd start giving Carol more of the attentive demonstrations of love she craved and she would reciprocate with gestures of affection that would make some men's toes curl. Eventually though, they'd feel smothered by her constant demands or angry at not being loved for the person they were. Carol was desperate by now, at 33 the husband and children she dearly wanted were nowhere on the relationship horizon.

With careful exploration of her relationships, Carol began to understand how she was trying to force men to match her puzzle piece. With time she began to accept that she'd need to be open to loving a good man for who he *was*, without wanting to force him into the relationship puzzle she expected. It didn't mean she had to accept someone second best, she simply had to stop trying to force them to play her father's role. She needed to stop seeing that role as the only possible, successful role for her man to play. Only a few months down the line, Carol began her first truly fulfilling relationship. She met a man with many wonderful qualities who she could accept as a person in his own right. Carol had truly broken free of feeling she had to have someone identical to her in terms of relationship needs. His puzzle piece didn't have to be identical to hers.

# Finding A Complementary
# Puzzle Piece

If, at this level of relationships, you are looking for a puzzle piece that *matches* yours, you will rarely succeed! Can you imagine trying to force two identical puzzle pieces together into a fit – they simply won't go. The essential key to understanding the concept of the relationship puzzle is to look for a puzzle piece that *complements* yours. Finding a man who complements you completes the puzzle. His piece of the puzzle is *not* the same shape as yours. And you do not try to force him into an impossible shape!

The importance of understanding this concept develops both the theme of understanding yourself, and the needs, wishes, and desires that drive your pursuit of relationships. And how you look at men and understand them as potential partners, too. As you read through the case studies – real experiences of real women – in the coming chapters, you'll see me come back many times to how important the concept of the relationship puzzle is.

# Beginning To Find Your Relationship Potential

So let's begin by taking the first step to having a successful relationship. And that is to give up searching for a man 'like me'. This means not expecting him to feel like you, think like you, or act like you in your relationship. And not changing him either! Of course you expect him to behave well, respect you, and love you, but he isn't you! Start searching, instead, for a man who complements you. This means exploring a man's qualities, personality, and differences and seeing how they fit with you and your life. The way he feels, thinks, and acts in terms of romance and intimacy is different from your way of feeling, thinking, and acting. This should be viewed as a positive. The two of you with your unique outlooks can complement each other's lives. Absorbing this concept is the first step to finding happiness in your romantic relationships.

##  The Goldilocks Syndrome – The Trial And Error Approach To Relationships

I'd now like to introduce another essential concept that will also be referred to throughout *You & Him*: this is the 'Goldilocks syndrome'. Think back to the childhood fairy tale about Goldilocks. She was desperately looking for comfort – something to fill her stomach and somewhere to lie her head.

Goldilocks tried the various bowls of porridge and different beds, looking for something comfortable.

Think of yourself and other women you know – have you, and they, pursued many relationships to find one with a comfortable fit? Have you tried one, only to jump up because it didn't 'feel' right? Have you moved on to the next relationship only to find the same thing? In the end, have these relationships finished because you weren't comfortable and decided to move on? Or because you were chased away by an angry man – perhaps because you'd been trying to mould him to your puzzle piece? This is what I call the Goldilocks syndrome where women hop from relationship to relationship without enough thought about *why* their expectations aren't being met. Like Goldilocks, they simply hope for a fit as they dip into that new 'bowl of porridge' or sit and test that 'new bed'. In the end, hope is a good thing but it is not enough!

Now there is nothing inherently wrong with such a trial and error approach to relationships. At least there isn't if you happen to stumble across one that works for you. But in reality this rarely happens. And it's far better for your emotional well-being to take a positive and proactive approach to finding a good relationship. The key is to understand why you have been driven to try out relationship after relationship, meeting man after man but never really connecting with any in a genuine manner. What are your expectations that are not being met?

How do you act at an emotional level towards the men you meet?

##  The Six Goldilocks Styles

It is my firm belief that there are a number of 'Goldilocks styles'. These emotional styles keep women locked into certain patterns of behaviour. Too many women continue to function within these basic styles, even when they repeatedly fail to find happy relationships. They have little success because they don't understand why they're doing what they're doing at a romantic level. They simply continue to behave, and feel, again and again in the same way, in the same style, with different men, and expect it to work. They fall back on their style, like a bad habit, with every new man they meet. Sometimes, though, romantic intelligence and success comes when, like a sunrise slowly bursting onto the dark morning sky, women develop awareness and understanding of their own style and how it may be holding them back from their relationship potential. This is how I hope understanding will dawn with you – as you read about and identify your own style!

Identifying your own relationship style is critical to understanding yourself and is an important piece of the relationship puzzle. If you know *why* you behave, and feel, in certain ways, and have particular expectations within romantic relationships, then you can put this knowledge to use – just as

Carol did! You can choose to alter a relationship style that is preventing you from finding real happiness. Or you can move forward, within your style, understanding the implications of your choices and behaviour – helping you get to the heart of your relationship potential.

The six basic Goldilocks styles are described in chapters three to eight. Each of these chapters will conclude with a quiz or dilemmas to help you decide how high on the scale you are for each style. You may find that more than one of these styles seems all too familiar to you and reflects different aspects of your emotional self. That is not unusual as we, as women, are complex in the way we face the romantic possibilities that come our way.

 # The Next Piece Of The Puzzle – Your Relationship Pattern

Before we get down to the important business of identifying your 'relationship style' in chapters three to eight, you first need to be aware of your 'relationship pattern'. Your relationship pattern provides the basic structure to your relationships. Your pattern is your basic relationship history – have you had lots of short relationships right in a row? Or have you had a few long-term relationships? Perhaps you've woven an unpredictable relationship history – sometimes having flings, punctuated by the odd long-term relationship? Your pattern is the punctuation to your relationship style. The style being the emotional filling to your relationship history.

Your pattern forms another piece of the puzzle. Typical patterns are fully described in chapter two. Understanding your relationship pattern, and then your style, can help you break free of any unfulfilling cycle you find yourself in. These unfulfilling cycles become a broken record of unhappiness influencing all your actions and expectations. You get stuck in a groove, repeating the same unhappy note over and over. Instead of repeating the same relationship mistakes, the understanding you develop will help you jump off this broken record.

##  The Men You Meet

And now, how about those all-important men you meet? The second part of *You & Him* will give you important insights into the way men actually approach romantic relationships. Again the concept of the relationship puzzle will feature frequently, particularly in the case studies described. This is where your romantic intelligence will really start to take off and develop. It will help you develop an understanding of men, and their differences, which will greatly increase your chances of finding the right relationship. Once in that relationship, this understanding will help you enhance the quality of it. Many more pieces of the puzzle will fall into place in these chapters.

Instead of being perpetually surprised by the behaviour of men 'in love', you'll actually be able to enjoy the knowledge you will develop. You will no longer feel undermined by what you have taken in the past as his non-committal, or puzzling, approach. You will also not be troubled by the sometimes apparently simplistic nature men have. You know what I mean – sometimes men seem so straightforward, we actually can't believe there isn't something more going on in their thought processes! Especially when our own thought processes are working overtime at a million miles an hour trying to figure something out in the relationship.

In the past, you've dug around deeply trying to decipher what his simplistic responses actually mean. You try to delve into his psyche hoping to find out what he really means by the things he says or does. And very often you've looked for complexity that simply is not there. Instead you will genuinely be able to gauge his level of romantic interest and commitment. This combined with awareness of your own pattern and style will help you to decide whether or not this is a man, and relationship, that's going to go somewhere and is worth working for.

# Enhancement Strategies

As you read through the women's stories included in *You & Him*, you will come across exercises that have helped these women improve their romantic relationships. These are my personal enhancement strategies (PESs) and romantic enhancement strategies (RESs). The basis for PESs and RESs were to give these women specific goals to achieve. And in achieving these goals, they gained more control over the progress of their romantic relationships.

You might wonder why I have included PESs. That's because in getting to the heart of their relationship potential, women very often need to enhance the way they feel about themselves at a personal level. The way you feel about yourself does have a direct influence on the 'you' that you bring to relationships. If you bring a 'you' that lacks confidence, is self-doubting, pessimistic, or vulnerable to a relationship, you may well jeopardize the success of that relationship. I'd like you to use any of the PESs and RESs you feel apply to your needs and romantic life. You will also come across relationship enhancement strategies when I discuss cases from couples' work in Part II, *Understanding Him*. These strategies may be used with a partner if you are currently in a relationship.

Finally, you are reading *You & Him* presumably because you want to get more from your intimate relationships. Within every woman there is great capacity for change and development. If what you've been doing in the past hasn't worked for you – that is you are not in a happy relationship at present or haven't been happy in past relationships – then you can choose to do something about it. The emphasis our society puts on having a fulfilling, successful relationship puts this right at the core of our feelings of success, or failure, as a person. You can feel successful and develop a happy relationship, both by understanding yourself and understanding men – it really is possible!

Part One

# Understanding

# You

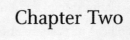

Chapter Two

# Typical Relationship Patterns

What's Yours?

Now we are ready to begin a journey of understanding *you* and the sort of relationships you've been having! I frequently find that when it comes to affairs of the heart, women often develop blind spots in terms of what's actually occurring, even in the most intimate aspects of their lives. You've undoubtedly noticed when a friend seems to be missing the obvious – like failing to see the man she adores as the two-timing cheat that he is. As their mind races with thoughts of the man in their life, they don't actually consider the nitty-gritty of how the relationship is building up or where it's actually heading. The pieces of their relationship puzzle are scattered throughout their mind – many of these having to do with their romantic history.

It's very often the case that women think of the overall picture on the front of the puzzle box before they've even had a chance to look at or think about the pieces. Questions like 'Could he be the one?' and, 'Will this relationship be the one that really works?' cloud the more basic issues. These thoughts drench them like a beautiful cascading waterfall of romance. Where do all these thoughts land, though? In a great big splash around their feet. Rather than starting from these grand, all encompassing questions, I advise women to slow down and come to terms with the pieces that will eventually go to making up the whole romantic relationship.

You may ask why it's important to think in terms of bringing together the pieces that go to forming a relationship and analysing them. Isn't it more fun to have dreams of a fairy tale wedding in mind by the third date? (As you are reading *You & Him* I assume you are interested in the long term!) Or how about visions of him with two little kiddies bouncing on his knees by the end of the first? Maybe it should be taken as a sign of optimism that someone is considering the big picture, you think. And you would be right, if you were talking about a woman who had enjoyed some tremendous romances, knew exactly what she was looking for, and had terrific levels of confidence in her judgement. But it's rare to come across someone who has enjoyed absolute bliss with men. It's far more likely you'll meet women who've had a few romantic 'ups', many more romantic 'downs', and who've been around the block a few times but still can't find their way to the next street!

When talking to women I find they devote a lot of time to thinking about men. But very often these thoughts swim randomly through a romantic haze of hopes, dreams, and yearnings. Fantasy and dreaming are fine to a point – after all they make romance fun. In the longer term though, they won't get you as far as a real understanding of why you've had the sorts of relationships you've had. And what this relationship history means to your romantic future. If you really do hope to end up with that idyllic picture like those on the fronts of puzzle boxes, it's time to start sorting through the pieces properly.

 # Understanding Your Relationship Track Record

So where's the best starting point for understanding your own relationship track record and what this means now? From experience, I've found it's important to begin by looking at your relationship pattern. Your relationship pattern provides the all-important punctuation for the emotional flow of your relationships. Think of the pattern as the road along which your relationships have travelled. It may, for example, be punctuated with lots of stop signs. So as noted in the introductory chapter, this shows you've had lots of short relationships coming to a stop quickly. Understanding your relationship pattern will help you understand the flow of your emotional life. If you've had problems finding fulfilment in your relationships, then identifying the pattern you fall into may help. There are five basic patterns I'd like to illustrate for you.

##  I. The Avoidance Pattern

Let's begin with the avoidance pattern. Have you ever known women who never seem to get off the starting block with men? Their relationships seem to end before they ever get going. Some negative emotional force seems to hold them back from really enjoying being with a man. In the chapters to come you'll see how different relationship styles could lead to this pattern. These women have plenty of opportunities but never seem able to seize them. And once this pattern sets in a sense of emotional isolation develops. This compounds the problem and sets the pattern in stone. Of course the pattern may vary, for example, from a woman who can flirt but never accepts a date to one who has a couple of dates and backs out.

# Jenny's Experience

I was struck very strongly by the avoidance pattern when I first met Jenny. Jenny was a tall, striking looking twenty-something who looked like she 'had it all'. In fact Jenny did truly seem to have it all in terms of style, personality, and a fun job. She seemed busy socially with friends and different interests. But in fact what Jenny had never had was a real boyfriend.

Of course she'd experienced a few flirtations. Jenny could recall in amazing detail flirting with potential boyfriends in the office and at social gatherings. But she'd never managed to get off the romantic starting block with anyone. She complained of bleak feelings of isolation and hopelessness in terms of her future. When I met her she was quite depressed. Friends and acquaintances making choices to get married or at least experimenting with cohabiting confronted her on a regular basis. She felt like a romantic oddity compared to most people she knew. Jenny also felt she could never really join in her friends' conversations about men, as she believed she had nothing to add. And although she'd once experienced a one-night stand with someone she'd met at a very drunken Christmas party, she certainly felt she could never join in conversations about more intimate topics like sex.

As an 'avoider' Jenny was left feeling excluded from so much of what she saw around her. As we talked about her relationship history, it became clear that she had never got past the point of 'romantic possibility' with men. By 'romantic possibility' I mean that delicious point in the interaction between two people when it becomes apparent they are interested in each other at a level more than friendship. It is that moment when awareness dawns of new and special elements entering the equation. Elements like sexual chemistry, a desire to know more intimate details about each other, a blinkering to others outside the two of you, and an urge to make extra effort to get to know this new person.

People at the point of 'romantic possibility' are transparent. They've suddenly got a buzz about them, a new, daring hairstyle, and a spring in their step. This is the moment when most intensify the attention they pay to the other. But for Jenny, with a classic avoidance pattern, it was the moment she backed off.

Much of Jenny's romantic behaviour also tied in with her relationship style. However, in this chapter I am simply trying to convey to you the importance of identifying and understanding your pattern. Jenny's avoidance pattern may sound as if it would have been obvious to anyone who thought about it. This is not necessarily the case though because avoidance patterns can sometimes be camouflaged. For example, a woman with this pattern may be incredibly creative in the reasons she comes up with to justify why she hasn't taken the plunge after the first few meetings. With each man, there's a new reason why he wouldn't be suitable to date any further. You can guess the kinds of things, from silly reasons – 'He has a ridiculous laugh, I know it'll drive me crazy!' – to vague ones – 'I don't think we're thinking in terms of the same things!' And just what 'things' does she mean? Mortgage repayment schemes? Garden furniture? Until you've given someone a chance you can't make these judgements.

Another tack avoiders take is the one regarding 'things' in their own lives. These excuses are also varied. They range from the ridiculous – 'I can't start seeing him as I've got a course of dental treatment starting,' – to the pragmatic – 'I can't start dating that other guy because I'm busy changing jobs.' Whatever the reasons, and as you read through the coming chapters on relationship styles, you'll come to see there are many possibilities, you can bet you're dealing with an avoider when the reasons begin to sound hollow or always come at the same point in a fledgling relationship. Usually when it's simply a spark in that new man's eye!

## The Avoidance Dilemma – What Would You Do?

Jane met a man, Tom, over the fax machine at work. They had similar level jobs but in a large company so that they didn't have to cross paths very often. Jane was struck by all the great

qualities Tom seemed to have. They started an email relationship and had met for a couple of coffees. With time though Jane
felt some of what Tom included in his emails was too personal.
She decided she didn't want to date him after all. What would
you do if you were Jane?

A) Jane should email Tom that things have got on top of her at
   work and she can't handle any 'distractions' right now.
B) Jane should give Tom more of a chance because on email
   sometimes the meaning of things seems more abrupt or is
   distorted.
C) Jane should ask Tom what he meant by his emails – if Jane's
   happy with the answer she should keep seeing him.

**Dilemma Decision:** In selecting **A** it probably won't come as a
surprise to you that you have avoidance tendencies. Choice **A**
illustrates a desire to sweep things under the carpet or make an
easy get away. Unfortunately when you make that sort of choice
with a new romantic interest you may be missing out on all
sorts of possibilities. And you are not allowing yourself the
opportunity to communicate openly. If you selected **C**, you are
the least likely to act like an avoider. This choice demonstrates
your desire to face romance straight on so that you can make
sound judgements! Selecting **B** would mean you are most of
the way to facing the difficulties in new romances. But you'd
need to find the confidence to look for more clarity as situations arise.

**II. The Butterfly Pattern**

You've undoubtedly heard of the term 'social butterfly'. The image conjured up by this is of someone who flits around seeking social enjoyment and pleasure wherever offered. There is a lack of stability but presumably a lot of fun by seizing every opportunity presented in their social life. Imagine this in terms of romance. The butterfly pattern is found in women who have multiple relationships at the same time. That might sound like an enviable place to be in modern life – you could pick and choose which man to see on what evening. A real 'If-it's-Monday-it-must-be-Mark,-Tuesday-it-must-be-Tony' scenario!

However, women with the butterfly pattern do not usually devote enough emotional energy to any one man to make the relationships work. This usually ends up in emotional confusion and turmoil – these women ask themselves: 'What am I doing wrong when I meet so many men but never end up in a happy relationship?' The problem lies in spreading themselves so thin at an emotional level that everyone involved ends up feeling cheated. The reason why they do this, of course, depends on their relationship style.

Although some women have success with the butterfly pattern, this is usually due to having reached a certain point in their life. For example, it may be a time when they've moved home or jobs and are meeting loads of new men, and dipping their toe into many romantic ponds at once. This is fine and eventually they may reach their relationship potential when the time is right. But for most women this pattern leads them to being over-stretched emotionally. They cram as much dating in as possible. But dating requires valuable emotional energy and a woman may find she doesn't have the resources to cope! Of course this pattern will suit those men who don't want a relationship – the ones simply looking for fun without strings attached. This pattern means you aren't able to make many demands on them because you don't have enough focus to do so.

 ## Cindy's Experience

Cindy was a very pretty woman who seemed to have a constant stream of male admirers. Yet as far as her girlfriends were concerned she always seemed to be moaning about her love life. They got fairly sick of hearing her complaints. They'd say things like: 'You've captured the attention of so many men – now do something about one of them!'

Inside Cindy felt incredibly lonely and very angry with herself. She knew she actually shared so little at an emotional level with each of the men in her life. Through her sadness, she also began to feel she was incredibly selfish. Particularly when friends would tell her to stop complaining as she'd dated half the men in her local area. Even though it had always been like this, Cindy had failed to identify herself as a butterfly. She was getting to burn out stage and wanted help.

##  The Butterfly Dilemma – Which Choice Is Yours?

Let's use Cindy's situation for the butterfly dilemma. The final straw was when someone she really liked, Jake, called it off with her. Jake told Cindy that he'd really wanted to get something started with her but was finding it impossible. Jake described how Cindy's love of the outdoors and great sense of fun had really sparked feelings in him for her. But he wanted a 'one-man woman' and it obviously wasn't going to be Cindy. Cindy was very unhappy with this news.

What would you do if you were Cindy?

A) She should ask Jake for more time while she tried to sort out her feelings.
B) It's obvious Jake's not the one for her. Otherwise he'd be prepared to give her more of a chance.
C) She should let Jake go and take a breather from seeing men. She'd need to learn to say 'no' to impulses to date every man who crossed her path.

**Dilemma Decision:** If you chose **B**, you are most likely to have butterfly tendencies yourself and probably recognize this! By

jumping to the conclusion that Jake's not the one, you are showing the impulsive butterfly pattern. From all accounts he has
given Cindy time (and chances) – he knows about her interests
and obviously has awareness of the number of men in her life.
Choosing **C** would indicate you are least likely to think like a
butterfly. Clearly Cindy does need to undergo some emotional
recovery and you've judged this correctly. In order to break her
butterfly pattern, she needs to go 'cold turkey' for a while and
that even means letting go of Jake, and all the other men in her
life. The answer **A** isn't quite going far enough to sort out this
pattern. Cindy shouldn't have the pressure of Jake waiting
around for her. Instead she should independently examine her
choices in her own time and space as in choice **C**.

##  III. The Serial Fling Pattern

You've seen how the butterfly pattern doesn't allow any real
emotional connection to develop. It's the same with the serial
fling pattern except for different reasons because the pattern is
different. A woman with the serial fling pattern gets involved
with a series of men one after another. Although she is essentially a 'one-man woman', unlike the butterfly, no emotional
depth is ever achieved in any of these flings. A constant
longing develops for emotional nurturing which is made impossible by the short-term nature of the flings.

This pattern allows the woman to get off the relationship starting block, but for her own unique reasons (whatever her style), she's unable to sustain these. It may be for reasons like she expects 'too much, too soon' or she's frightened of losing emotional control, that will be covered in the chapters concerning relationship styles. Whatever it is through, friends and family may come to worry about her relationships being shallow.

 # Linda's Experience

Linda, 28, is a woman I met who was having difficulties with her family over the pattern of her relationships. They were concerned at her constant stream of boyfriends that seemed to lead nowhere. She felt a lot of pressure from her parents to settle down. Linda was the only one of her tight-knit group that was still single. After a particularly nasty argument with her mother, Linda decided to seek help with her relationships. Whereas before she'd blamed her parents for being old-fashioned and too involved in her life, Linda now questioned her own judgement about relationships.

Like the proverbial penny that seems to drop from out of the blue, in talking she suddenly realized just how predictable her relationship pattern was. In the past, you could say Linda had a bit of romantic 'amnesia'. Very convenient – particularly when people don't want to remember bad behaviour or face reality on their part! When discussing her relationship history, she would've brushed aside her parents' suggestions that she seemed to be on a treadmill of throwaway relationships. She simply couldn't see how predictable her pattern was. Overall each man was allocated about a dozen dates. Usually Linda would sleep with them around the third. She'd start expressing doubts about the ninth and finish it at that dangerous dozen. Now she was prepared to admit she needed to change this pattern.

You must have had friends whose mothers have thrown up their hands saying, 'When will any of her relationships last?' Very often friends and family will try to set these women up with someone, muttering, 'She simply needs to find the *right* man to stick with,' – when it's usually *her*! And these women end up envying the depth of some of the relationships they see around them. Especially as they seem so near to getting a relationship off the ground, and yet frustratingly far.

### The Serial Fling Dilemma – What Do You Think?

Susan has had at least eight flings in the last two years. She has a true serial fling pattern. This has given her a bit of a reputation at work as a woman who has to have a man in her life. Each time she meets someone new, she dives in with huge optimism thinking she'll make it work. Susan is always making comparisons between the new man in her life to the last.

Sometimes it's favourable: 'At least Steve doesn't expect me to sit through football with him like Ben did!' Sometimes unfavourable: 'I wish he could be more like Sean was in bed!' What would you do if you were Susan?

A) The next time I was tempted to get involved with someone, I'd slow down and get to know him at a friendly level first.

B) I'd only date men who friends or family set me up with.

C) I'd make an effort to look at each man as an individual when I started to date him.

**Dilemma Decision:** If you chose **A**, you are unlikely to fall into the serial fling pattern. This demonstrates awareness that the key to Susan breaking such a pattern lies in two areas. First to slow down – very important for the serial flinger who just can't be without a man in her life. And secondly to get to know someone first as a friend is valuable with Susan's history of packing men in so tightly that she can't help but compare each to the last (or even the last few!). She'd be more likely to judge them as individuals. The answer **B** implies you'd be most likely to think like a serial flinger, which you probably had already guessed! If Susan simply gave up responsibility to her friends and family to find men for her, she may still remain in this pattern. This action would be unlikely to solve her problem. Choosing **C** is more helpful as it shows you understand the importance of looking at each man as an individual. But you're still not reaching the level of answer **A**.

**IV. The Serial Monogamist Pattern**

When we hear the word 'monogamy', we think of enduring, committed relationships. But of course some people think 'boredom'! They're the ones who haven't reached the settling-down stage or have flea-like patience. It's not all clear sailing as many women struggle with a number of long-term, yet unsuccessful relationships. They fall into the serial monogamist pattern. From the outside it looks like they've got it made. They've had a number of relationships – so they didn't settle for the first man who came along. They've had long relationships – so they've probably got to do all those things we hope we'll do with a man one day. Things like being loved for ourselves, warts and all, developing silly pet names for each other, talking about the meaning of life, and what we'll be like together at 70. You know what I mean!

Others will look at these women and wish they had a track record like that. It's human nature – we're always comparing ourselves, sadly. A habit we should all break! When talking 'shop' with friends, which means talking 'men', you'd assume they'd hold the higher moral ground – after all their long relationships at least demonstrates staying power. But unless they've been one of the lucky women who have a number of successful long-term relationships, you have no idea what these relationships have been like. Think of the worst case scenario –

many women in abusive relationships are those with the longest staying power; they are frequently serial monogamists!

Whether or not these relationships can be characterized as a success depends on many things. A frequent problem, for example, is women who play 'house', even as adults. You know the game we all play as children and always argue about who plays 'mum', 'dad', or 'baby'. Although they have long relationships, they simply play at them. They may coast along, allowing the relationship to drift, and never reach the level of intimacy they'd like to. This, of course can be very deceptive to those looking in. The biggest clue, giving away a serial monogamist, is long-term relationships characterized by one over-riding and not particularly positive attitude. This attitude could be jealousy, possessiveness, or the opposite – a blasé attitude, or ambivalence even. And this attitude largely depends on their relationship style.

 **Angela's Experience**

Angela, 45, described to me a classic, unhappy, serial monogamist pattern. Since her mid-twenties, she'd had five long-term but extremely unhappy relationships. Each lasted about two years. Angela sat in front of me describing a feeling of complete emptiness and a nagging suspicion her excessive drinking was a means of swamping this lonely feeling. She felt she couldn't turn to friends about this because she had always played along in her relationships, never really allowing anyone to know her innermost feelings. When I asked her why these relationships all seemed to end at the two-year mark, Angela described how she'd reach bursting point and would simply have to finish them. Evidently to friends, she'd explain that she wasn't quite 'ready to commit' and it wasn't 'fair' to each man if she let it go on any longer. Angela had now lost the optimism she once had that she could gain real intimacy with a man – what she wanted most and everyone assumed she was achieving. She felt she was nowhere near reaching her relationship potential.

This pattern probably leaves women in the most danger of friends or family not understanding what's gone wrong. For the very reason that it looks like they're having romantic success. And if for whatever reason they're not honest with those close to them, it's unlikely that this will be guessed. With this in mind, it's easy to see why women with this pattern are potentially the most vulnerable to long-term feelings of failure.

**The Serial Monogamist Dilemma – How Would You Handle This?**

Jasmine is in the second year of her most recent long-term relationship. She's beginning to feel it's going 'nowhere' like the last. The main problem seems to be Jasmine's jealousy of the social life Jim's workplace gives him. They end up suffering long silences when she gets angry. If she was honest with him, it's been crossing her mind for the last couple of months that 'time is up', and believes she should probably finish the relationship. What would you do if you were Jasmine?

**A)** If I'd been thinking about it, and my feeling was to move on, then I'd probably be right.

**B)** Jasmine needs to discuss these negative thoughts she's been having with Jim immediately.

**C)** Jasmine should try and break her pattern by hanging in there longer with Jim.

**Dilemma Decision:** If you chose **A**, then you're most likely to think like a serial monogamist. They have the tendency to keep their innermost thoughts to themselves. If these thoughts are ones that could influence the long-term success of the relationship, then they must be discussed openly. Selecting **B** would indicate you're least likely to act like a serial monogamist. You realize the importance of facing up to feelings that left without investigation can fester. Many serial monogamists playing at relationships haven't discovered these skills. The choice C, although showing optimism, doesn't allow for truly facing up to the feelings and how these can affect the relationship.

##  V. The Erratic Pattern

At some point everyone encounters a woman with an erratic pattern. You can't miss them – they stick out a mile away. This is the completely unpredictable woman that appears to be leading an exciting life from the outside. If you know her for a while you may marvel at the way she seems to have flings, and then settles down for a while, followed by a period of romantic abstinence where she can't seem to get anything off the ground with anyone. She's actually great to have late-night girls' chats with because her life has been one great theme park of romantic adventure. Like any child, she has visited all the rides!

If you look closely at her relationships, though, you'll usually find she's bouncing between the alternatives without much control. The excitement of the 'erratic' experiences in her early years of dating usually leads to her getting her fingers burnt in every way possible later on.

# Valerie's Experience

A woman I spoke to recently, Valerie, was in quite a desperate situation by her mid-thirties. No matter what she tried, and she had tried it all, rarely had she enjoyed any pleasure in her relationships. Whatever she was experimenting with – trying to hang on to a relationship for all she was worth, to flirting disastrously with any single man she met – it never went the way she wanted.

Valerie had fallen out with her best friend for having a fling with her friend's brother. Her friend thought her brother was worth more than that. She had gained a reputation in her office after having a long, tempestuous relationship with one of the managers. When it ended, everyone held their breath to see what the atmosphere would now be like. And now she'd argued with her older brother. In a protective way, he had tried to discuss her personal life and Valerie had told him to butt out in a non-protective way.

When women 'try it all' and still meet without success, you'll know they are an erratic. You may assume such a pattern is always highly visible – exciting and adventurous – but this isn't always the case. Some erratics quietly go about their romantic experiments and don't necessarily follow Valerie's example – falling out with all concerned. And others quite frankly have fun when their pattern is based on simply taking life as it comes and enjoying it until they decide they want to settle down. As with all the patterns, the success or failure depends on the style and the emotions driving them!

## ♥ The Erratic Dilemma – What Is Your Solution?

Liz has just had a few flings and she's feeling rather 'burnt out'. One fling was with a work colleague but at least they've both got over the uncomfortable feelings they had when the fling first ended. The other two were with men she'd met at a singles group. These had followed fast on the heels of two long-term relationships. Neither of which survived her relentless pursuit of perfection. She's now toying with the idea of dating a man she's been introduced to by a friend. Nick seems stable, hardworking, and down to earth. Liz thinks that Nick will be 'just the tonic' she needs. What would you do if you were Liz?

A) I'd steer clear of Nick as a friend had introduced him, and I'd be wary of upsetting the friend if it didn't work out.

B) As Nick has such obvious good qualities, I'd ask for a rain check. Right now I think I'd rather not jeopardize dating such a catch when I'm not ready.

C) If I, too, thought Nick would be a tonic I'd date him. He could be good for me.

**Dilemma Decision:** Choosing **C** would mean you have an erratic way of thinking. Needing a man to be your tonic will never work and is definitely a dubious way to approach relationships. Emotional stability must come from within. This will then lead to romantic harmony. The **B** answer means you have the least tendency toward having an erratic pattern. It's absolutely good romantic sense to put off dating someone who might be special when you've just come out of a string of different relationships. In choosing **A**, you've demonstrated you're not ready to see someone who's been introduced by a friend. You know you still may have problems with your pattern but haven't suggested any solution like **B**.

 # Using This Puzzle Piece

Now the five main relationship patterns have been introduced. Have you been able to identify your pattern? I'm sure there will have been a feeling of identification with one or another! At this stage, this forms the first big piece of your own unique relationship puzzle. Using this knowledge will help you get to the heart of your relationship potential! Next we turn to your relationship style. Your relationship style directly relates to the emotional issues driving your romantic behaviour and intelligence (or lack of it!). Learning about the styles over the next six chapters will help you identify another important puzzle piece.

## Chapter Three

# Goldilocks Style One

Recreating Your Parents' Relationship

I bet you've never thought you're anything like your parents in terms of romance. In fact the thought of your parents getting romantic and having an intimate relationship probably makes you say, 'Don't *even* go there!' in true American talk show style. We tend to repress any such thoughts, as face it, we're selfish – 'mum' is mum and 'dad' is dad, and not each other's lovers and life partners. However, it is absolutely the case that we learn about relationships from our parents. And if not both our parents together, as divorce has been common now for years, then the one who has the most influence over our emotional development. The relationship they share with each other, or new partners if divorced, serves as a standard for our own, the style of romance we understand.

You may not be consciously aware of this influence – until now. And even now you'll be thinking sceptically, 'How on earth am I like them? They're so old and romance was so different then!' Yes, certain aspects of romance have changed: like romantic etiquette that used to be very clear and is now completely confused – who does make the first move nowadays? But for the most part, relationships still have the same qualities they've had for generations.

For most women, it takes careful exploration of their upbringing and present relationships before they see the connection. But at the very core of your emotional self, there is an echo of their image reverberating around inside of you. The strength of this echo, balanced by the level of awareness you may have about learning from your parents, determines how far you try and recreate their relationship within your own. How far you are prone to the first Goldilocks style. Exploring this possibility will help you reach your relationship potential. Understanding the extent you may function in this style forms another piece of your puzzle. Are you a Goldilocks who looks for porridge that tastes like mum's and a bed that reminds you of home?

# Typical Recreating Behaviour

💜 You hear her say 'He's just like my dad!' Or, 'If only he could be more like my dad.'

💜 She sets about making her home resemble her parents'.

💜 She takes pleasure in doing things 'just as mum and dad did'.

💜 She sticks rigidly to family traditions.

💜 She finds it hard to acknowledge that she's driven to be like her parents at an emotional level. Even when a boyfriend is breaking up with her complaining, 'You're just like your mum!'

# Where Does This Style Come From?

💜 So how exactly does living with your parents' relationship affect you? Let's begin with the basics and take an example with a rosy glow. If every morning at breakfast, your mum and dad made tender remarks to each other, offered to make each other toast, and exchanged a warm kiss goodbye on the doorstep, then you'd come to think that this is the way parents *are*. As parents *are* this way, then that's the way you'll *be*.

- Now for another example: let's say every morning you woke up to find your father on the couch, having been kicked out of the bedroom. Your mother's face is tear stained as she prepares breakfast and there is an icy silence as they leave the house. This happens day in, day out as you grow up. And you'd come to expect this from relationships!

- With such a negative style of relating being presented in the latter case, you may ask why any child would go on to recreate it? Because we all buy into the myth that mum and dad are the most powerful people in the world (at least until we're older when it dawns on us parents don't know everything!). As we think they know what they're doing, so they must be doing something acceptable. Deep down inside, like some emotional river that flows from generation to generation, your expectations are formed.

 ## The Main Reasons Why This Goldilocks Style Will Stop You Reaching Your Relationship Potential

- Some women do question the relationship style their parents had, allowing them to make their own decisions about how they'll live with their partner.

For others, they don't learn as they grow up that their relationship should suit their lives, their feelings, and needs. Instead they are fixed on recreating their parents' relationship – the style they feel comfortable with. Their style of interacting with men becomes one that drives them towards having what their parents had.

💗 Sometimes this gets into the complex area of trying to fix what at some level you believe your parents did 'wrong'. By choosing a man like your father and, at a subconscious level, trying to shape him into the man your mother wanted, and now you want. In these cases you inherit the battles your mother fought – and either won or lost.

💗 Many women find disappointment in this quest to replicate their parents' relationship – most men don't want to be forced to play a role that isn't them!

💗 There are other forms this Goldilocks style takes. For example, a woman may truly long for the relationship her parents had – even when her life's completely different. She may try to reproduce the relationship by acting as her mother did and looking for a man like dad. Or again trying to get a man to fit into dad's role. Alternatively they try to recreate the father-daughter relationship in a similar fashion as Carol did, described in the introductory chapter. So much romantic energy is wasted, and pain caused, in these pursuits.

## When This Style Might Be A Success

This style can work when your parents were happy and presented you with a positive relationship model (so you're not trying to right their wrongs). And when the man you fall in love with shares your desire for the sort of lifestyle you want (the one your parents had). This set of circumstances will help you get to the heart of your relationship potential.

 # Tanya's Experience

I met Tanya when she was 37 and just going through her second divorce. Tanya was an emotional mess and the divorce itself was not a pretty sight. She and her nearly 'ex' were at the 'I-wish-he/she-would-drop-down-dead' stage. It didn't matter they had a lovely child to nurture, or a newly built home to sort out. They were simply at each other's throats and trying to get back at each other.

What had caused such a break down in six short years? From Tanya's point of view, Richard had become uncaring and unfeeling – devoid of any of the emotions he'd once had. From Richard's point of view Tanya was 'mad'. A great deal of talking uncovered the simple fact that Tanya had wanted to recreate her parents' relationship down to the finest detail – to every last echo from her past. She'd insisted they had the same style luxury estate car her parents had (even though Richard could not really afford it). The same springer spaniel dog (even though she never walked it) and dreamed of the day they could have the large house and garden her parents had.

This sort of pressure, over the years, had been like Chinese water torture. The drip, drip, drip had caused enormous resentment in Richard. He was seething, but as much with himself as with Tanya, for having put up with it. He could, after all, have said 'No' to the spaniel, which he knew she'd never look after, or 'No' to the car with the crippling payments. In his own way, he'd allowed Tanya to try to rebuild the relationship of her parents. And Richard had come to the point he felt unloved. Tanya didn't want him, she wanted the 'dream' of her childhood.

Tanya had taken his resentment as a sign that she somehow wasn't worthy of his love. This was after all her second failed marriage – was she unlovable? Her self-esteem was at rock bottom, only matched by the intensity of her anger towards him. However, talking gave rise to the real reason. She was simply driven by a deep-seated need to have what her parents did. This was particularly intense due to her being an only child. They had heaped their expectations on her. Tanya had accepted this pressure unquestioningly. And at every level of her life, she was trying to live up to their expectations with disastrous consequences for her romantic life.

We identified her pattern as an erratic pattern. In her pursuit of her parents' relationship, she'd been through flings, one-night stands, punctuated by long-term relationships (the two marriages). Her parents had laid her personal unhappiness at the door of her 'erratic behaviour' as they described it. They certainly hadn't seen she was desperately trying to satisfy this unspoken need.

##  Tanya's Dilemma

The dilemma I posed Tanya quite early on was this: if she were allowed to tell her parents only one of the following important messages, which would she choose?

**A)** I'd like you to know how much I've always admired you.

**B)** I'd like you to know how hard I'm trying to sort my life out.

**C)** I'd like you to know how I'm learning to be myself.

**Dilemma Decision:** If you thought she should choose the first then you may have recognized her tendency to let her parents' expectations swamp hers. If she had chosen the last, this goes furthest in conveying a sense that Tanya is coming to terms with her world. An important developmental step that should have happened years before. Most of us separate from the major influences of our parents by our early 20s at the latest.

In discussing these choices carefully, Tanya began to realize the meaning that lay behind them. And what her choice said about her. That to put her admiration for her parents above everything else meant she would strive and hope to be like them possibly to unreasonable levels. Which is exactly what she'd been doing.

Tanya quickly realized she'd been locked into this Goldilocks style of trying to recreate her parents' life. Treating each man as a piece of pliable clay that she would try to sculpt into someone who'd give her the relationship echoing her parents'. Angering each man along the way. Now she realized why her relationships ended with such anger! Tanya set about learning to expect the unexpected, and not feeling she had to live by some set of inherited expectations. She also set to work trying to change the way she treated men.

Other forces shape the romantic knowledge we take away from our parents, too. And this adds to the complexity of our behaviour and feelings. These forces include the first romantic relationships we have. You may meet and date a young man who has a completely carefree attitude to life. From this you learn to act spontaneously when with him – you know the sorts of antics some teens get up to. They suddenly decide to scale the tallest landmark in sight to see what it's like kissing up there! As if air quality changes kissing quality! With another, you may find he's very controlling and tries to force you into living up to his expectations. These first romantic encounters can alter our original version of what romance should be like.

With Tanya's intense style, though, the men she'd met hadn't stood a chance of altering her version.

Another influence is what happens to our girlfriends when we're in our teens. All those late night 'girlie' discussions and zillions of phone calls back and forth that drive our parents mad and shape our views. 'Haven't you just seen Sally at school already today? Can you not live another moment without touching the phone? Is it some sort of breathing apparatus for you?' they ask with exasperation. During this period, such input from friends can help us learn there are other ways to have relationships. You may watch Sally completely dominate some poor boy. He follows her around like a lost puppy. This makes you realize there are some men who'll be putty in your hands, too. Even if your own father could never be described as 'puppy-like'!

You may not end up attracted to a male version of the doormat, like your friend Sally. But this knowledge will affect your deepest feelings about the rules governing relationships. Of course the original set of rules being learned from your parents. Even our parents' relationship may change over time and with circumstance. And we can benefit from their new experience and find this affects our beliefs.

# Sharon's Experience

Sharon's case illustrates how wanting to 'fight your parents' battles' leads to unhappiness. She desperately wanted to correct the 'wrongs' in her parents' relationship, wrongs that had partially been responsible for her father's suicide when she was 15, to satisfy some deep emotional need. From her earliest memories, Sharon could recall terrible arguments that seemed to revolve around her mother's constant demands on her father. Her initial impressions as a young girl were that men were weak. At least her mum was always ranting at her father that he wasn't strong enough to provide the sort of lifestyle she 'deserved'.

As Sharon grew older and started dating men, she always seemed drawn to emotionally unstable ones. What at first she saw as a 'gentle' nature, that somehow gave her a comforting feeling, later she saw as weakness. The style her relationships took was directly influenced by the echoes from her childhood and was like this: first there was a sense of optimism – 'I can look after this man.' As things progressed, these men would increasingly irritate Sharon. 'Why can't they stand on their own two feet?', 'Haven't I given them enough backup?' she'd ask herself. At this point the arguments would start. Towards the end, Sharon would find impatience she didn't think she was capable of and was particularly vicious until they would leave. She'd drive them away. An echo of the way her mother (at least partly as he had other problems too) had driven her father away – to suicide.

When I met Sharon, she was on the verge of total despair. She had some understanding that somehow she treated men the way her mother had her father – a thought that mortified her. And she hated herself for feeling so optimistic and truly in love in the early days of relationships and then allowing them to end in such terrible ways. It seemed beyond her to create the happy ending, which deep inside she wished her parents had experienced.

First we clarified her relationship pattern. Sharon was a true serial monogamist. She had real staying power in her relationships, but for the wrong reasons. One at a time, she'd devote herself to them. Deep down she longed for each of the waifs and strays she dated to stand up and become the confident, 'go-for-it' man she wished her father had been. Sharon hung in there for many months on average, even when the anger and viciousness set in.

Careful exploration allowed Sharon to recognize her deepest, yet unfulfilled, wish. This was her feeling that if her father had been that way – confident and 'go for it' – he'd never have resorted to suicide. The most important goals for Sharon were twofold. To learn to contain this 'need' to correct the wrongs of her parents' relationship. And to accept the next man she dated for himself. Not to expect him to be a puzzle piece in the shape she wanted!

##  Sharon's Personal Enhancement Strategies

The PES I felt would benefit Sharon most was to undertake a series of writing tasks to help her define herself. Any woman too immersed in recreating her parents' relationship style needs a stronger definition of her own personality. These tasks included:

- Creative writing – writing a letter to a fictional employer in a 'caring profession' describing herself. Sharon was to stand outside herself and write the description as if it were from a friend. I chose the caring profession as this would require a fairly personal description.

- Personal opinions – on a daily basis Sharon was to write down one opinion she'd had. This could be about anything – from an opinion about a politician in the news to one about the lurid dress sense of her employer. She was then to 'respect' this opinion – praise herself for her point of view.

- Letters to a loved one – perhaps the most painful task, but I now felt Sharon was ready, was to write to her dead father. This was to describe her shattered hopes, her recollections, and her feelings about the place she wished he still occupied in her life. It was to conclude with at least two positives, or happy endings. Possibly the hope she'd recently developed, for example.

## Sharon's Romantic Enhancement Strategies

- ♥ Romantic opposites – I asked Sharon to make a list of all the opposites a romantic relationship could have, compared to what she recalled of her parents'. Her list included <u>respect for each other's feelings</u> (because her mother certainly had not respected her father), <u>taking responsibility</u> (because her father allowed this to slip through his hands), and showing affection. When asked which was the most important in *her* eyes, she chose 'responsibility for yourself'.

- ♥ Encouraging romantic responsibility – Sharon's goal for the next date she had was to let the man take responsibility for himself in *all* ways. At all costs, she was not to accept a date from a man where her instincts told her she wanted to take over. You may think this is rather harsh on the guys that struck her as weak. She could give them a chance, stand back, and allow them to take responsibility. However, until she could prove, by dating someone who didn't appear 'weak', that she was letting go of her damaging style, she should avoid such men.

- ♥ Accepting your own path – Sharon drew a time-line of her relationships and studied the pattern. With each failure, she marked how it had gone wrong by trying to recreate her parents' relationship. Sharon could see in front of her that accepting her own needs was going to be the key to romantic success. She no longer felt compelled to treat men as her mother had treated her father.

QUIZ
## Are You A Goldilocks In Search Of Your Parents' Relationship?

I would like to help you identify to what extent you may be falling into this Goldilocks style. Answer each question honestly even if you realize what the implications are!

**1  Do you ask your mother for advice about men?**

   **A**  Frequently – she always seems to be right about men

   **B**  Sometimes – if I think she understands the man I'm seeing

   **C**  Rarely – I'd be more likely to talk to a friend

**2  When interacting with your partner have *you* ever thought, 'I'm behaving like mum!'**

   **A**  If I'm honest – yes, frequently

   **B**  That thought might cross my mind

   **C**  No, I think that would be unlikely

**3  What statement best sums up the way you feel about your parents' relationship?**

   **A**  I've always looked up to them

   **B**  I've not really explored my feelings about their relationship

   **C**  I've tried to look at their relationship in a balanced way

**4** **Has a partner ever accused you of being like your mother?**

A  Yes, most likely in the middle of arguments

B  On occasion

C  No, or yes, but not in a negative way

**5** **Have you ever pressured a man to be someone who 'fits in' with your family more?**

A  Yes, it's caused quite a few arguments with men

B  Sometimes I've felt this way but not really acted on it

C  No, I'd hope my family would accept him the way he is

**6** **Have you ever thought in terms of your partner reminding you of your father?**

A  Yes, it's uncanny

B  Sometimes I've had thoughts like that

C  If I did, I would think carefully about what it meant

**7** **Have you ever been described, or described yourself, as a 'daddy's girl'?**

A  Yes, many times

B  It was suggested by someone

C  No, definitely not

**8** **As a child, hearing your parents argue, did you think, 'Mum's right, why doesn't dad listen?'**

A  Yes, I would always think that

B  Sometimes I'd think that

C  Not necessarily

## GOLDILOCKS KEY

**Five+ As** – you have a strong tendency towards recreating your parents' relationship! Have a careful think about this. Are you trying to recreate the relationship your mother and father had? Or are you trying to recreate the father-daughter relationship? Try the things Sharon did which may apply to you. The following may also be helpful in breaking free of these chains from childhood:

### Key romantic message = Live your own life!

- When you meet someone, avoid dating him if you feel a strong pull to shape him into your father.
- If you catch yourself about to sound like your mother, then change what you're going to say, or how you're going to say it.
- If the new man you meet makes you feel like you want to change him to fit in with your family, then he's probably not a good bet for you.
- Look at potential partners for the men they are. Do the qualities they have seem positive?
- Beware of falling into the trap of expecting your adult life to be like your parents' life.

**Five+ Bs** – you may have some tendencies towards this Goldilocks style. Think carefully about this if you find yourself in unhappy or unfulfilling relationships. You may be trying to force a man to fit into recreating your parents' relationship with you.

**Five+ Cs** – it appears unlikely that you are trying to recreate the sort of life your parents' had. You think for yourself and would be able to put echoes that linger from childhood into perspective. You may of course recognize yourself in some of the other relationship styles as you read through the following chapters.

**Final thoughts** – if your parents enjoyed a happy, contented relationship, then you're going to expect the same level of happiness for yourself! However, you have to ensure that the men you meet are looking for a similar relationship and lifestyle. What you view as fulfilling (your parents' shared love of tending their garden in a golden haze of contentment, wearing matching sun hats, chatting animatedly about this year's growth), he might view as boring (he may not want to spend his life gardening with you!). Or in one of many other ways not right for him. It is the emotion – happiness – that is important. The mechanics of achieving this (gardening, salsa dancing, continual communication, or leaving each other alone!) will vary between couples. Drawing together your understanding of a man's expectations in this context is one more puzzle piece. Expectations of happiness come in different shapes and sizes. Forcing a man into fulfilling your need to recreate your parents' relationship is bound to be fraught with problems!

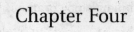

Chapter Four

# Goldilocks Style Two

## Giving Up Responsibility
### (IJH – 'It Just Happened')

Has anyone ever described a scene along these lines to you –
'I couldn't help it – it just happened – I slept with my cousin's
boyfriend!' (Or 'My sister's ex-boyfriend', or 'My ex-boyfriend's
brother' – you know the kind of thing I'm getting at!) And they
continue along the lines of, 'I know it's wrong but it started
with simple flirting at a party. Of course I'd had so much to
drink, I really didn't think it would go that far. When he invit-
ed me back to his place, you know, it just happened!' Did your
jaw drop open at the feeble nature of this excuse for such bad

behaviour? At the time you may not have challenged her about her bad behaviour. Instead you thought, 'What an awful situation to be in!' And if you did challenge her, it was probably along the lines of, 'How could you let something like that happen?'

'It just happened!' or IJH as I call it, is something I hear frequently in talking to women with relationship problems. In fact it becomes the battle cry for people who want to place the blame for unhappy relationships or circumstances they find themselves in on anything but themselves.

They don't accept responsibility for their romantic entanglements. They blame some particular set of circumstances – being pressured, or vulnerable, or even drink as in the example above – for choosing inappropriate men. Or for having affairs that have no chance of working, and repeatedly finding unhappiness or no real intimacy. Imagine Goldilocks simply dashing about tasting porridge and testing beds and then denying she had any choice in the matter! These women taste and test relationships without playing a real part in them and never reach their relationship potential.

These romantic choices usually lead to low self-esteem that may take on complex forms. The woman starts to feel ineffectual and questions her abilities. She may begin to feel childlike and that somehow she needs to be taken care of. Worse yet, she may think someone who is able to take control of the relationship should dominate her. Breaking free from this Goldilocks style involves creating an upwards cycle. As self-esteem increases, and the ability to accept responsibility, so you are less likely to choose men who fit your expectations that nothing is within your power. Your choices will start to work for you, rather than against!

 # Typical IJH Behaviour

- ❤ She won't acknowledge responsibility for mistakes.

- ❤ She easily allocates blame for things that happen. Like blaming the man when a relationship ends.

- ❤ She's likely to make unscrupulous relationship choices – like seeing attached men.

- ❤ She makes claims like: 'I'm having fun so what does it matter?', 'I go with the flow.' The war cry of: 'It just happened!'

- ❤ She may not be the most reliable friend.

- ❤ She may need baling out of trouble she's caused at parties, in bars, or even in the office!

# Where Does This Style Come From?

♥ Women who have been pampered by their parents often don't learn to take responsibility for their behaviour – and this extends to their romantic behaviour. If they've been spoiled, it usually means things have been handed to them on a plate. This means they may simply expect things to happen in a relationship. But when you are relating to another grown-up (at least some men are!), they may be expecting you to take your fair share of responsibility and not simply drift along.

♥ Women who've been disappointed in the past can decide to give up trying. Their attitude becomes: 'If things haven't worked when I've tried hard in the past, why bother now?' They become quite neglectful of themselves emotionally. And any romantic optimism fades. Essentially they're romantic 'quitters'. This can lead to an increasingly downward spiral.

♥ Women with low self-esteem often feel they don't really have any choice when it comes to romance. Their standards are low and they end up taking what they can get. If you're giving off a message that says you don't really care about yourself, you will be the perfect target for men who either want to control you in the long term or simply use you for short-term fun. It's also likely you won't have the assertiveness skills essential to having a proactive attitude towards romance.

 # The Main Reasons Why This Goldilocks Style Doesn't Allow You To Reach Your Relationship Potential

- Women who fall into this style tend to find it hard to make decisions when it comes to affairs of the heart. They could be the most high-flying businesswomen, but they are unable to act in a positive manner when it comes to their romantic relationships. This will drive men to distraction; most want a woman who knows her own mind.

- They're frequently buffeted between strong emotions. One moment they really can't live without this new man. The next moment they can't be bothered to return his calls. Because they're not being proactive they tend to be rocked by the normal doubts most of us face up to and try to sort out. And they are also swamped by the strong emotions that occur naturally in a relationship. Particularly when these occur in the early stages when the chemical reaction is likely to be highly charged. These emotions and attitudes can be hard for a man to understand and decipher.

♥ They are easy targets for men who may not have the best intentions where relationships are concerned – like married men! They wrestle with strong feelings between their consciences and letting such a romance develop. And as with many women faced with choosing to have an affair, or not, they may genuinely weigh up the pros and cons, but then still simply go with the flow. They go with the pressure he puts on to have a little 'fun'. The fact they fancy someone who is decidedly off-limits will be put to the side for the moment. After all why take responsibility – shouldn't he?

 ## When This Style Might Be A Success

The IJH style is most likely to succeed when a paternal type of man wants to look after someone. No matter how much progress has been made in terms of women being viewed as able to stand on their own two feet – some never will! Let's be honest, though, there are plenty of men who can't stand on their own, either! It can also work when, with perseverance, a man encourages an IJH woman to gradually build up responsibility in a relationship and get to the heart of her relationship potential.

# Cindy's Experience

Cindy is a good example of a woman with low self-esteem, who was prone to falling for married men. She'd given up all responsibility in her relationships by the time we met. At 24, she'd been involved with about half a dozen married men. Friends had commented on her repeated mistakes. Cindy would simply shrug her shoulders and say, 'They just seem to happen that way. I only seem to meet the married ones.' This surely was a case of IJH!

Of course Cindy had a choice in the types of men she dated and the relationships she had. But her inability to take a positive stance in her dealings with men meant she slipped into these relationships without thinking. And she was particularly vulnerable working in the male-dominated environment she did.

Now though, it was one married man too far – trouble brewed. His wife had found out! John was in a panic and dumped Cindy so fast she hardly had time to draw breath during his parting words, 'Don't ring me whatever you do!' The emotional whirlwind left her reeling and without much sympathy from friends. They had a 'told-you-so' attitude that if you play with fire (and married men were 'hot'), then you're likely to get burnt.

Cindy and I talked a great deal about where her IJH came from. Why did she simply let relationships 'happen'? It became clear she had never developed very high self-esteem. Her mother had raised her single-handedly after leaving her abusive husband. Cindy had many recollections of her mother 'putting herself down'. Even though Cindy loved her mother dearly, her mother's own low self-esteem was contagious. She had caught a massive dose of it that stopped her reaching her potential.

We also identified her serial fling pattern. Cindy only got involved with one man at a time. But these never turned into fulfilling relationships – how could they, they were with married men – they never lasted past four or five weeks. Add the fact that she gave up responsibility in these flings, they certainly had no chance of developing. They were furtive, they were fast, but they weren't forever. This pattern was leaving little room for emotional recovery between the flings. I felt Cindy would benefit most from a positive, problem-solving plan of action. Enough talking had been done – she needed to take action, even if only in small steps.

## Cindy's Personal Enhancement Strategies

It was important that the basis for Cindy's PESs was to learn to take responsibility for herself. And that meant being positive about herself! This would enable her to build the necessary self-esteem for taking responsibility in relationships.

♥ Be positive – first Cindy made a list of her positive attributes. With careful consideration, we explored at what points
in her day she was vulnerable to 'running herself down'. It
transpired when she faced certain tasks she felt daunted
(especially since she often left them until the deadline was
upon her making matters worse) and would lack confidence. I had her tape this list inside the relevant filing cabi-
net drawers. When she had to face those difficult tasks,
she'd also have to 'face' her attributes. Cindy was to repeat
them to herself and then progress with the tasks.

♥ Inner voice – we then worked on her 'inner dialogue' that
was incredibly negative. Cindy took a dictaphone and when
alone, she simply spoke into it – all the things from her
'inner dialogue'. Her 'running narrative' was quite amazing.
With almost every turn her mind made, self-doubting statements would creep in: 'Why did I say that?', 'Did he understand what I meant?', 'God, I look awful today!', 'I can't
cope!', etc. It was difficult to weed out any positives! With
such extensive negativity, it's best to start small. Cindy
chose to begin with any inner comments regarding her
appearance. If 'I look a mess,' crept into her mind she was
immediately supposed to substitute it with something like:
'I actually have an amazing smile!'

♥ Negative generalizations – the more difficult areas included the generalizations she would think in, for example, 'I
can't cope!' These needed challenging rather than simple

substitutions. When a thought like that raced through her mind, she had to stop herself and challenge it. She'd think things like: 'Actually I've got through a huge amount of work this week!'

💝 Validation from others – Cindy made another list of all the positive or complimentary things people had said to her in the last few years. She was not to be embarrassed by this task. Instead she was supposed to feel good about it! Cindy wrote out things like the times her boss had told her 'well done!' and when friends had said how great she was.

💝 Taking responsibility – Cindy's final but equally important PES was to be on guard for any part of her life where she gave up responsibility. If a friend said, 'What movie should we see?' she was not to say, 'I don't know!' Instead she was to make a choice wherever possible.

## 💝 Cindy's Romantic Enhancement Strategies

Cindy needed to completely rethink the way she faced men. The PESs I gave her would help her develop responsibility within relationships. The RESs would develop this further.

💝 Enhancing romantic self – the first applied to her inner dialogue in terms of men. She needed to start believing she deserved better relationships. She chose some simple self-affirmations to think about every day. These included: 'I only deserve the best!', 'I don't need men and I want to *choose* to be with them!' And, 'I won't put up with any bad behaviour!'

- 💗 Visualization – Cindy then tried a visualization of the sort of man she'd like to meet and relationship she'd like to have. I asked her to think of this RES as if she were creating her own romantic movie in her imagination. She was to run this 'film' a couple of times a week. It wasn't supposed to be like a cheesy 'B movie' but a realistic interpretation of what would make her happy. In her 'movie', Cindy also found it helpful to think of a part that she'd seen an actress play that she admired in terms of romance. She chose Meg Ryan in *Sleepless in Seattle*. Cindy saw herself as a warm, funny woman enjoying a relationship with a kind, intelligent man.

- 💗 Recognizing weakness – Cindy's next RES was to recognize signs of weakness. First within herself and second in the men she met. For example, if she was having a bad day and a married man from work started to flirt with her, she was to remove herself from the path of temptation. If she recognized weakness in a man, like building his ego up with inappropriate flirting, she was to believe her intuition that he was unlikely to have a positive effect on her.

- 💗 Romantic responsibility – Cindy was to again take responsibility in dating situations. She was to give her opinions, make choices, and set boundaries. Even the simplest decision, like what time she'd meet for a drink, was to be hers.

With time, Cindy began to take a much more positive approach to life. Although she had the occasional slip-up (like flirting with a married man at one party), she never actually went into another painful relationship. This piece of her puzzle had sorted itself out – she understood the style she'd been operating in. She couldn't give up responsibility for choosing the men to get involved with ever again.

Whatever the reason behind your IJH, like Cindy's low self-esteem, it may end up with the same result. It's exasperating for men to start a relationship with a woman who seems unable to participate fully. Unless they want to take advantage of this!

 ## Alison's Experience

Alison's story demonstrates one of the other reasons – when a woman has been disappointed. As a 20-year-old she had met and fallen for a much older man. He seemed so different from all the students she'd been dating. They all seemed immature compared to Matthew. Although her parents objected to Matthew's age, for a number of months things seemed to work.

Matthew then began to treat her with disdain around his friends. As if she was some 'toy' he'd outgrown. He'd put her down and tell her how naïve she was. Instead of finishing with her, he let it drag on. Alison found this slow, breaking-up phase devastating. Until the end, she clung on to the hope that it would work, that their age difference didn't matter, and he'd stop undermining her. But she'd given up responsibility for her own wellbeing in the relationship by allowing Matthew to treat her badly.

When the crunch came, Alison had a 'revenge' fling with one of Matthew's recently divorced friends. Joe, being on the rebound, thought it was great to have a fling with someone younger. It was a mind-blowingly passionate fling. Joe was in 'I'm-back-on-the-market' mode and Alison was 'I'm-in-getting-back' mode! When Matthew found out, there were fireworks. Each of them had arguments with the others. But much to Alison's disappointment, boys will be boys and stick together. Joe and Matthew made it up while leaving her in the cold.

Alison then essentially gave up on relationships. She'd been alienated from a lot of her college friends during this time, so she didn't have much of a support system. Her parents were so relieved the older men were out of her life that those feelings of relief prevented them understanding her pain. She had recently developed a close-ish relationship with a male college tutor, ten years older than herself that felt quite comforting.

# ❤ Alison's Dilemma

If you're likely to give up responsibility you may recognize which solution Alison wanted to choose.

❤ Alison should avoid the tutor at all costs. That way she won't be tempted into having a relationship with someone she shouldn't (someone who has influence over her college course), and once again giving up responsibility for making good choices.

❤ Alison should allow herself to get to know the tutor better. By testing herself she may find the tutor proves to be a positive 'experiment'. She can be around older men but not have to fall for them. He can become a good role model for her – that not all older men are b*******.

❤ Alison should stay with her tutor but keep the relationship formal. This will give her a new found control over relationships where, in the past, she may have been tempted to make questionable choices or go with the flow to a dangerous extent. Group tutorials may be the best way for keeping it on a formal footing. Alison should remind herself that a feeling of 'comfort' needs to be appropriate. Does this 'comfort' refer to 'academic encouragement'? Or to a more 'intimate emotional comfort'.

**Dilemma Decision:** Choosing the first is going too far. It doesn't present a learning opportunity for Alison – that she can take control of relationships, academic, emotional, or otherwise. The middle choice is the least helpful. Alison shouldn't put herself in a 'test' situation prematurely. At this point Alison is very unsupported by friends or family. Therefore this choice allows the tutor to become a tempting emotional crutch – once again providing the opportunity for giving up responsibility. The most positive choice is the last. Staying with a tutor she feels comfortable with will be helpful academically. However, keeping it 'formal' will help her avoid slipping into an inappropriate relationship.

Alison came to accept that just because her relationships hadn't worked in the past (I got her to stop using the word: 'failed'), it didn't mean she should stop caring about future ones. As she regained her confidence, her life improved across the board. She got re-involved with student life and had a positive outlook to her studies and the future. Alison had pieced together an important part of the puzzle – your present and future relationships can be very different from your past – you simply have to make them different! She was fighting her old Goldilocks style of IJH and going to reach her relationship potential.

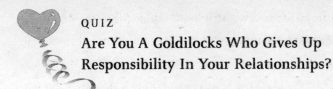

QUIZ

# Are You A Goldilocks Who Gives Up Responsibility In Your Relationships?

Please answer each question in the way that most represents how you feel.

**1** I am most likely to be the last one to make a menu choice when out to dinner

Agree/Disagree

**2** I find making decisions frightening

Agree/Disagree

**3** I am likely to get emotionally involved without realizing it

Agree/Disagree

**4** I sometimes wonder how I've ended up in some of my relationships

Agree/Disagree

**5** I am likely to make inappropriate choices like seeing a married man

Agree/Disagree

**6** I sometimes feel like a 'lost little girl'

Agree/Disagree

**7** My boyfriends are likely to complain that they have to make all the decisions

Agree/Disagree

**8** I simply like to let a relationship take its course

Agree/Disagree

**9** I let men take the lead in bed

Agree/Disagree

**10** I think it's probably the guys' fault that my relationships don't work

Agree/Disagree

**11** If a man pressures me enough, I'll go out with him

Agree/Disagree

 ## GOLDILOCKS KEY

Three to six 'agrees' — you are vulnerable to suffering from IJH! It's time to change today!

Seven or more 'agrees' and you definitely have an IJH relationship style! You probably keep seeing men who fit into your relationship style and allow you to give up responsibility. And if they don't want to take responsibility from you, then they've probably found it very difficult trying to have a relationship with a woman who can't handle her share of it! Try the following to break free from the IJH style and get to the heart of your relationship potential:

## Key romantic message = Take romantic responsibility!

Choose carefully who to go out with. Don't say 'Yes' to anyone who is pressuring you, or makes you feel uncomfortable in anyway. For example, if they make you feel like a little girl. This may indicate they want to take over for you and run your life.

Completely avoid inappropriate relationship choices like seeing married men. And this means not even meeting them for a coffee or drink!

Take responsibility for yourself in all areas of your life. This includes things like if your parents spoil you – show them you've grown up. Your behaviour will speak louder than words. If one area of your life is successful, like work, transfer those responsible behaviours over to interactions with friends and men.

When someone asks for your opinion or choice – give it!

If they don't ask, but you're dying to have 'a voice' then volunteer it!

Don't let alcohol, or worse – drugs – loosen your old vulnerabilities. Don't over indulge on dates. The more in control you are of your faculties, the less likely you will be to go with the flow – in a dangerous direction.

All these steps will help you become a woman who can take responsibility in her relationships!

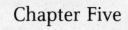

Chapter Five

# Goldilocks Style Three

## The Need To Control

Have you ever felt a little anxious that something wasn't quite going your way in a relationship? Perhaps the new man in your life seemed to enjoy – too much – his nights out with friends. Your inner dialogue started to work overtime as you wondered quietly about the following sorts of possibilities: 'Is it that he simply doesn't want a serious relationship, so he doesn't want to see me too frequently (that's fine as long as you don't waste time)?', 'Maybe he doesn't find me stimulating enough to spend more time with (help!)?', 'Worse yet, he might be playing the field and seeing other women on his nights off (horrors!).'

This feeling, you may recall, wasn't very pleasant. And so you fretted about it and possibly talked to friends about how to work this out. In the end, hopefully through a combination of your own judgement, getting to know him better (and so what he was looking for), and piecing things together, you worked out what was happening. The sense that things were out of your control, subsided like a thundery storm that drifts into the distance as the sun starts to shine again where you are.

Now take those anxious feelings that you managed to overcome and magnify them a hundredfold. Imagine feeling that way all the time in relationships. Not having enough faith in yourself to sort things out. Not having the courage to face relationship hurdles in a positive way but instead feeling you have to control every last detail so that things go *your* way. Not a very nice emotional place to be! This is how a woman with the third Goldilocks style feels. That unless she controls every factor in her relationships, they will be out of her control – out of her territory and in some unknown and frightening place. It's like Goldilocks deciding she must control the state of the porridge in each bowl and the cosiness of each bed or she won't be happy! After a while your emotional resources are stretched to the limit and such a relationship style leads to burn out!

This chapter examines the relationship control freak – the opposite problem to IJH! This style is governed by your fear of losing control and so you take *all* the responsibility for a relationship.

 # Typical Controlling Behaviour

💗 She complains that the new man in her life is 'difficult' or 'won't fit in with her'.

💗 She spends enormous energy organizing every detail of her life – including her dates.

💗 She is short tempered when things don't go her way.

💗 She has quite a pessimistic outlook on life – everything is futile because people don't think the way she does!

💗 She is bossy even in platonic and female friendships.

💗 On breaking up, she's liable to say that she 'tried everything' to make it work.

# Where Does This Style Come From?

💙 Early family experience that consisted of a lot of change. If change isn't dealt with positively in the family, it may leave you with a sense of nervousness about keeping things the same. This then leads to a need to control events and people as far as you can manage.

💙 One or both parents had obsessive tendencies that you learned. Women with obsessive personality types are very prone to being a relationship control freak. If you have a tendency to obsess about your work life and home life, you may be vulnerable to being an obsessive in love. And now it appears more likely there is also a gene for obsessive behaviour. You may have inherited this!

💙 The whole pattern of obsessive behaviour revolves around issues of control. There's a strong need to control everything in your life so that you feel secure. Such women find it difficult to relax and enjoy the moment. Their relationships may lack spontaneity and unless the man wants to be controlled, they will find it very hard to handle. Even so, once recognized women can actively start to relax, one step at a time, and enjoy romantic attachments that are more fulfilling and less controlling. Not based on an obsessive need!

- Past emotional trauma that has left them with a need to leave nothing to chance – in any part of their life.

- Just as some women who have been let down simply give up in future relationships – like Alison in the last chapter – others become obsessed with controlling the next man in their life. So it's not necessarily a case of always having been obsessive! Once they've experienced the anxiety and fear that can result from romantic trauma, some women go on a mission to prevent this ever happening again.

 # The Main Reasons Why This Goldilocks Style Will Stop You Reaching Your Relationship Potential

- Some women who have this relationship style do not trust their partners to fulfil their part of the bargain. They can't 'let go' and this drives men away who want to be trusted and can take responsibility!

- They may find men who fit this style and can't take responsibility. They are controllable. Eventually they see these men as weak and lose respect for them.

- Or because of their single-mindedness, they try to take control of men who don't fit into this style to mould them into someone who suits their needs. When this doesn't succeed (if they've chosen a man with an ounce of self-respect!), they perceive these men as difficult.

💜 They meet controlling men who at first glance seem to be men who know what they want. This is attractive to the controlling Goldilocks types – at a subconscious level, they've selected someone like themselves. But put two controlling people together and there will always be power struggles!

💜 You may think that wanting to control things could be a positive in terms of relationships. The difference lies in taking responsibility for yourself – as you should – and trying to take responsibility for the man too – which you shouldn't! Finding this balance can determine the difference between having successful romances and having difficult and painful ones.

## 💜 When This Style Might Be A Success

This Goldilocks style may work with a man who is used to being dominated – a momma's boy – as long as she doesn't grow bored. It can also work when the two of you have similar needs to control, coupled with the same expectations. For example if your long-term game plan is the same, then you two reinforce each other in a positive way.

# Amber's Experience

I once met a woman, Amber, 39, who was desperately unhappy about the state of her relationships. Her brief marriage to Simon had failed after one too many jealous outbursts. Simon had said there was no chance of salvaging things. I asked her to describe what her relationships were like. She told me she always felt she was walking an emotional tightrope – one wrong move and she would plummet! The problem was by walking this tightrope and feeling she could never relax in her relationships, she was causing herself to plummet repeatedly – each time she was dumped.

Amber described her life-long jealousy over men. This took many forms. She was jealous when they had interests that didn't include her, but included others (like Simon and his football. He seemed to have so much fun with his team-mates). She was jealous if they worked with women (as is the case in most modern offices!). And she was jealous of time they spent with their own family. When Amber went into the detail of these feelings, it was obvious the jealousy stemmed from fear. If they weren't by her side, then she couldn't control what they were doing, thinking, or feeling. Something she tried to do with them that prevented her reaching her relationship potential.

With Simon she used to throw mini-tantrums when he went off to football or had to go out with colleagues. She hated herself afterwards, as she knew she was driving him away. But she couldn't stop. When she felt he wasn't doing as she wanted, it inspired incredibly strong feelings that burst out. In the end, Amber's fears were proved correct. Simon said he couldn't stand the way she tried to control everything and walked out. This was probably the seventh time she'd been dumped for these reasons.

In exploring Amber's relationship pattern it became clear she was a bit of a butterfly – at least until she'd married Simon. On many occasions she was seeing more than one man at the same time. Even then she still wanted to control them all. Amber could do what Amber wanted – they couldn't! The emotional energy she wasted was amazing. Dating two or three men every few months was exhausting. Her friends couldn't even keep up. But they were never surprised when Amber got dumped. They'd seen her in action – what man would want to put up with that?

On the occasions Amber did the dumping, it was because she had lost all respect for the men involved. With her pattern she had dated many men over the years. With these numbers, she was bound to meet a few who wanted to be dominated! Of course when she got this, she would tire of it. It was as if Amber needed the challenge of someone she had to mould, whose puzzle piece was nothing like hers and she was going to fight to shape it. It was too easy when the guys rolled over and played dead.

Where did this need come from? Amber's background sounded exotic but had actually left her prone to needing to control things. Her father had been an executive with an international company who'd been posted to highly paid jobs abroad. Amber and her family had lived a life of luxury but with a price. They never knew how long they'd stay in one country. Now this background could have resulted in a capable woman who could cope with anything. Or in a very laid-back woman. But the combination of her unique personality and the moving around had led to anxious feelings. These were kept in abeyance when everything in Amber's life was under control. She craved stability. Add a man into this equation – someone with his own ideas and lifestyle – and the out-of-control feelings quickly took over!

You might wonder why, when she met men happy to be controlled it didn't work. Just because Amber craved stability, this didn't actually mean she craved boredom. And these men, quite frankly, bored her. She as yet hadn't found that man – that puzzle piece – that complemented her. Because of her pattern (too flighty and emotionally over-stretched) and her style (too controlling), she wasn't likely to until she changed. Then she could allow a man, who wanted to play his part in a relationship, be part of her life.

# 💜 Amber's Dilemma

An 'ex' of Amber's, Alan, had phoned her recently. Amber had dumped him shortly before meeting Simon because he'd gone along with everything she wanted. In the end she wondered if Alan had any personality of his own at all. Now he wanted to try again. She wasn't sure what she should do. Even if you have controlling tendencies, you may have difficulty recognizing a controlling response:

- 💜 Amber should give Alan a chance. Maybe he's been working on changing just as she has.

- 💜 Simon has just left Amber so this is not a good time to try going back to an 'ex'. She may just use Alan for comfort and may slip into her old ways. She should give it a few months and call Alan if she feels like it then.

- 💜 Amber should try being friends with Alan. This way she can see if he's still the type to 'roll over' when ordered or if he's changed. If he has changed, she could then go out with him.

**Dilemma Decision:** The most positive choice for Amber is the middle. This is not a good time to see an 'ex', or anyone. When you've just separated, you tend to be needier than ever. This will just compound Amber's anxiety making her prone to controlling behaviour. The first choice may lead to this controlling behaviour. She's controlled Alan in the past and may try again now. The final choice is the one Amber, the controlling

Goldilocks, would choose and is definitely out. Now is not the time to play with a man's feelings. So testing Alan by playing at being 'friends' to see what he's now like is really using him. Amber will lose even more respect for him, if she feels she can play him along this way when she knows he wants to date, and not just be friends.

 ## Donna's Experience

Going overboard often results in more romantic trauma as Donna found out. When I first met Donna, I was struck with the vast amount of emotional energy that accompanied her every move. Now 29, at 24 she had been devastated by her then fiancé. She caught him being unfaithful in the bed they had shared! Worse yet, as far as Donna was concerned, Jason's lover was a man. Until this point Donna had experienced the normal range of romantic experiences – a little bit of heartbreak and a fair share of happiness. But this was outside the realms of her understanding. Donna felt she couldn't compete and she finished the relationship.

Donna had gone through a mourning phase swearing men were 'off the menu'. This didn't last long though and in the five years since the break up Donna has had three relationships. All of them have ended unhappily. Careful exploration uncovered the truth. Donna had become driven to control everything. The fear of the infidelity haunted her. She never wanted to experience anything like that again. This was complicated by feelings she had poor judgement (not suspecting her fiancé had bisexual tendencies).

This wasn't the full story because when I asked for details of the men she'd had the relationships with, it was obvious she had chosen relationship control freaks cast in her own mould. To Donna, initially these men struck her as people who knew what they wanted. It was obvious this was turning out to be an emotional euphemism for wanting things their way. So there would be Donna in her corner, determined she would keep a tight rein on the romance. And the men (one at a time!) in the other corner, equally determined. This emotional tension meant she never reached her relationship potential.

As each relationship started they seemed promising. Donna was confident she could stay on top of things. She also believed she'd chosen men who were her romantic equal. Unfortunately as she tried to shift the power in the relationship into her corner of the arena, they would try and shift it back. These subtle power struggles eventually became all out war. The break ups were mutual and destructive. Neither Donna nor any of her 'exs' escaped unscathed.

Donna's relationship pattern had always been one of serial monogamy. And really that's the way she wanted to keep it. Certainly at this point she had no interest in having flings and playing the field. Donna dearly wanted to find the right man to settle down with. Unfortunately this serial pattern over the last five years had been very painful. As each of the three relationships began, Donna would cross her fingers and hope 'this was it!' In the end her controlling style and choice of men who had a puzzle piece identical to hers (controlling!) resulted in failure.

##  Donna's Personal Enhancement Strategies

At the very deepest level, Donna needed to learn to trust herself again. In trusting herself, she could then let go of her controlling style. It was important she used PESs that would allow her to let go of the anxiety driving this.

- Extent of control – first we explored whether Donna's controlling ways were over spilling into the rest of her life. It was true, they had. Donna now found herself at work often anxious if her day wasn't going to plan. If it was 'moving out of her control,' as she described it, she fretted. A real waste of emotional energy! Identifying this over spill was important to helping her general wellbeing.

- Relaxation – next I encouraged Donna to visualize a situation where she felt very relaxed. Donna described a family holiday when she was about 16. She'd spent a week lying on a beach reading her first romantic novels. It was a golden moment in her life. No hassle, no strain! I asked her to put herself on that beach as she was now – the grown-up Donna. This was to be her relaxing image when she felt herself starting to 'control' things too extremely.

💜 Prioritize – each day Donna was to practise throwing her cares to the wind. She prioritized what was on her mind to 'A' and 'B' lists. 'A' list items/tasks were essentials and she was allowed to sort them out. 'B' list things were to be thrown to the wind! This was to be done either physically – like throwing out paperwork she would never get around to (things like filling in sweepstake coupons!). Or it could be done in her imagination. Donna was to have fun with an image of herself standing on a cliff top tossing away 'B' list items or thoughts.

## 💜 Donna's Romantic Enhancement Strategies

These RESs were used to help Donna allow men to participate in the relationship:

💜 Pacing – to feel less anxious about being in control Donna was to slow down the overall pace of her relationships. Rather than agreeing to three evenings out in a row, for example Friday, Saturday, and Sunday, she was to set a limit in the early part of the relationship. When not seeing the new man in her life, she was to keep busy, either by socializing with friends or enjoying a sport or hobby.

💙 Listening skills – Donna was to make a point of asking for the man's opinion or ideas every time she expressed one of her own. And then she was to listen to these, not simply pay lip service! To ensure listening she'd ask him more. She needed to build up communication where both she and the man had a say.

💙 Sensual visualization – because Donna hadn't been enjoying the sexual side of her relationships. (Would you if you were worried about controlling every last detail? Think of the things going through her mind: 'I've got to get the lighting right!', 'Is this too sexy, or not sexy enough?', 'I need to get him to kiss me longer,' etc!) She was to ensure she was relaxed before foreplay. Donna thought through a visualization of her sprawled like a starlet across the bed enjoying every moment. She was to take this image into her lovemaking. She also needed to avoid going to bed with a man until she trusted her feelings enough to let go.

💙 Reality check – if she felt a new man brought the worst out in her – her need to control things – then she was not to keep seeing him. Donna needed recovery time before she tested herself.

💙 Recognition – if she recognized controlling ways in a man then she'd be vulnerable to wanting to control back,

slipping into her old style. Either she was to set reasonable
boundaries with his needs, or not continue seeing him.

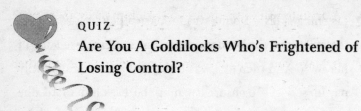

QUIZ
## Are You A Goldilocks Who's Frightened of Losing Control?

Choose the answer that honestly reflects the way you're most
likely to feel or react.

**1 Who do you think should make the first move?**

   **A** I always try to make the first move, or manipulate him
     into making it

   **B** Whoever has the confidence to make it

**2 Do you ever pressure friends into making decisions about
their romances?**

   **A** Yes, I love to give advice

   **B** I'd always provide a listening ear and give advice if asked
     for it

**3 Your lover suggests a new sexual practice; what would
you do?**

   **A** I'd probably need a lot of coaxing

   **B** I'd enthusiastically join in unless it was something
     really weird

**4** Your new boyfriend starts fixing the vegetables for your shared dinner his way, does this:

A Irritate you to the point you ask him to fix them your way?

B Make you happy for him to be involved or not bother you?

**5** If you're faced with a problem in a new relationship, how would you behave?

A I'd try to convince them to see my point of view

B I'd try to work it out together

**6** You don't like the way your boyfriend has arranged his furniture, do you:

A Set about rearranging it?

B Leave it alone?

**7** The man you're dating has a slightly annoying and loud laugh, how would you handle this?

A I'd drop major hints that he needs to be quieter

B I'd try to see it as unique and enjoy it

**8** Your boyfriend likes to spend lots of time playing a sport you don't like, would you:

A Try to get him to spend less time at it?

B Spend more time doing things you enjoy?

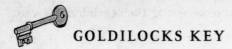

## GOLDILOCKS KEY

Five+ **As** – you probably treat men as a force to be controlled! If you haven't had much romantic success, it's probably because you keep trying to force men into fitting in with your relationship style. Or you choose men who give up responsibility and allow you to control the relationship. Neither of these will give you satisfaction so it's time to change!

### Key romantic message = Learn to let go!

Some things count in romance – like not letting a man treat you badly. Other things don't – like the way he laughs.

🔑 Explore where these feelings come from. Have you had a traumatic experience like Donna that's made you feel you have to be in complete control? Do you battle with jealous feelings like Amber, or perhaps other unpleasant feelings that fuel your controlling behaviour? Once identified make a plan to counteract them.

🔑 Learn to read your own signs of when you're getting near to a controlling episode. Do anxious thoughts start whirling through your mind? ('Why hasn't he phoned yet – he's really going to regret this!') Do you begin to feel edgy (gnawing on your fingernails and unable to sleep)? Identify these and then question them. Is there a more positive way of handling doubts, concerns, or getting your way?

- Always make a point of asking for his point of view and suggestions. Try to be fair. One night you choose where you go. The next date he chooses. Stopping yourself from taking over such practical details will improve your emotional outlook!

- Don't be afraid of spontaneity! Learn to seize opportunities and dates as they come your way. Don't be glued to your controlling routine.

- Let the past go. You can have balance in your relationships if you allow it. Trust your intuition about men and yourself. For example, if he seems like a womanizer, he probably is and all your controlling ways won't change him! If he acts like a momma's boy, then he probably will want you to take over from where she left off. Do you want a son or a lover? Once you trust your judgement you will look for a man who complements you, not one who needs controlling!

- In the end remind yourself of this question each day: are you going to control your part of the relationship? Or let negative emotions control you and the whole of the relationship?

Five+ **Bs** – you're unlikely to be vulnerable to this Goldilocks style. Keep balancing your needs with his needs, and your relationships stand a good chance of success.

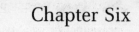

## Chapter Six

# Goldilocks Style Four

## The Relationship Terrorist

From time to time, we've all witnessed seemingly inexplicable behaviour in some of the women we have come across. Out of the blue a woman who has seemed happy, in what looks like an enviable relationship, suddenly dumps the guy. You're left thinking, 'If that was me, I'd have hung on to him for dear life!'

Then your natural curiosity for detail takes over and you ask her more about what's happened. She mentions reasons for finishing the romance that range from the odd to the obvious.

'He just wasn't really my type,' she explains. She describes how he would ask for other people's opinions about his haircut. An odd reason for breaking up you think! Maybe he wasn't confident with his sartorial style. Maybe his last girlfriend had criticized his hair and now he wanted reassurance. *You* would've given him a break over that one. Or she tells you how he couldn't put up with a little flirting – can't blame him for that, can you?

But not the relationship terrorist! This Goldilocks style is one of the most complicated. Men often complain they don't understand women but when they've experienced this style, they're liable to give up. Imagine that if Goldilocks had flung out all the bowls of porridge she'd tasted. Then she jumped up and down on the beds she tested. Such destructive behaviour would have frightened anyone off! But this is the norm for this relationship style.

You may even have been guilty of it yourself. Many women have behaved badly without letting it become a habit – or their relationship style. Perhaps you went through a bad patch after a particularly hurtful relationship. The next man who crossed your path was in for a rough ride. Usually though, having experienced the guilt that comes from treating an innocent man badly, we get back on track and don't become stuck in a destructive cycle. But not the terrorist who rarely reaches her relationship potential.

Sometimes when you cross the path of a relationship terrorist, they can seem quite fascinating from a voyeuristic point of view. They seem to act on a whim. Or behave a bit outrageously. It grabs your attention and you may even think, 'Wow, what an amazing, passionate love life she has!' But as you get to know a woman like this better, you see how very destructive this style is in the long run. It's destructive for the men involved – and face it they're not all bad! And it's destructive for the woman herself. It prevents any lasting relationship developing as important relational qualities like trust, respect, and affection don't have time to take shape. It leaves the woman, herself, with a tremendous emotional void to fill once the damage has been done.

 ## Typical Terrorist Behaviour

- Potentially there's a whole range of behaviour that could fit into this terrorist style.
- You will hear her say things like: 'I didn't think that would upset him!' ('that' being her flirtatious behaviour), 'I'm just not cut out for this relationship thing!'
- She is likely to be the life and soul of the party.
- She doesn't know when to stop teasing a man.

- When it ends, she's likely to blame it on the man for not being 'able to keep up' or being 'insecure'. (When really she's quite insecure inside.)

- You would never introduce her to your brother or male friends!

##  Where Does This Style Come From?

- Fear of intimacy is the main problem. Erratic behaviour, picking fights, and playing games can actually be signs of this. By jeopardizing relationships, they keep men at a distance. The relationship terrorist uses tactics bound to blow up in their faces. But at a subconscious level this is what they want. It prevents them from taking real risks by exposing themselves to intimacy. The first piece of the relationship puzzle these women have to work out is where their fear of intimacy comes from.

- Sometimes relationship terrorists love the risk-taking side of their behaviour. The thrill of not knowing whether they're pushing their present boyfriend so far that he might dump them excites them at some deeper level. They thrive on living on the edge until the day they take one damaging step too far and don't land on their feet.

- This style may be learned from having been raised in a chaotic family. You may have had friends as a child whose homes always seemed disorganized. They were never ready to leave for school on time, never had their permission slips for school outings signed by their parents, or returned library books on time. This unpredictable childhood environment leads to unpredictable adult behaviour.

- For whatever reason, they feel unlovable and behave in a way to make this a self-fulfilling prophecy.

 ## The Main Reasons Why This Goldilocks Style Stops You Reaching Your Relationship Potential

- Although initially fascinated with a 'terrorist' most men can't cope with the long-term challenge. What at first seems potentially a bit risky is soon viewed as dangerous.

- Because she's usually out of touch with her real feelings, even if she meets the man of her dreams, terrorists don't know how to cope. Although men are not necessarily the best equipped at handling their own emotions, they kind of expect women to handle theirs. When it becomes obvious she's can't, they worry about this unknown territory.

## When This Style Might Be A Success

This style will never be a success! Unless she meets a man open to a little emotional punishment – which is very unlikely! In its less extreme form, this style can work with men who are a little quiet. They bask in the reflected glow of their rather lively partner.

 # Carmen's Experience

Carmen presents the perfect portrait of a relationship terrorist. When I first met her at 27, she had broken so many hearts that she couldn't count them. Now she was reaching melt down. One part of her wanted to settle down but the destructive side to her nature overwhelmed that. She felt she had a constant battle going on inside her head.

Carmen would start seeing a man – being very outgoing she certainly attracted her share – and then have a fling elsewhere. Carmen's friends would often compare her behaviour to men. They'd say things like: 'You're always unfaithful – just like a man who can't keep his trousers on!' It was true – she'd never known another woman who'd betrayed so many men. Carmen would flirt, flaunt, and have the flings. The flirting would take place right in front of her boyfriends. She got away with it at first. They thought it was part of her larger-than-life character. Then, unlike most people who two-time, she'd actually flaunt her unfaithfulness. By flaunt, I mean she'd drop hints that she wasn't to be trusted. Men didn't know what had hit them.

Then it would become all too clear she was having a fling. Either they'd beg her to stop or dump her so fast she couldn't even say, 'Sorry, it didn't mean anything – it was just sex!' Now Carmen wanted to change. It was either that or get the ulcer she felt was beginning. Carmen also hated being ridiculed for being 'unstable' by colleagues at work whom by now were quite used to the amazing hurricane of her love life.

In talking about her family history it was apparent Carmen had grown up in an unstable household. Although her parents had never divorced, there was this underlying tension that it could all fall apart at any moment. Both of her parents were unpredictable with each other and this had a ripple affect on their parenting. If they were on an 'up', then the family would generally have a reasonable time. If her parents were on a 'down' though, everyone had to tread carefully. This disjointed style of family relationships left Carmen with little idea how to conduct a stable relationship. And certainly didn't provide a model for reaching her relationship potential.

It also emerged that Carmen identified strongly with her father. Secretly, as a child, she'd often taken his side in her parents' arguments. He was doting when he felt 'good' and Carmen loved this time together. But he also was easily flattered by the attention of other women. He was a great flirt and Carmen's mother was dogged by doubts – was he having affairs, too?

Whether it's nature or nurture – in Carmen's genes or in her upbringing – she had also developed this flirtatious manner. Combined with her inner sense that relationships are by definition 'volatile', she was on a collision course to unhappiness. Her pattern had the unpredictability of a true erratic. She would bounce from a few flings into seeing a number of men at the same time. This erratic pattern gave more explosive fuel to her terrorist style.

##  Carmen's Dilemma

Carmen had recently started dating a new man, Greg, who seemed down-to-earth and kind. He was obviously smitten with her apparent *joie de vivre*. Carmen was getting itchy feet, particularly as she was going on a training course where she knew there'd be lots of after-hours socializing. She didn't want to blow it with Greg, but feared her terrorist tendencies would overwhelm her judgement if she came across an attractive man. If you have terrorist tendencies, you'll probably recognize what Carmen would do if she were trying to be good:

💗 Carmen should avoid the training course if at all possible. Being placed in a situation where there may be lots of temptation is going to be hard for her. When she's feeling more settled she could go on a course.

💗 Carmen should discuss with Greg her feelings of having itchy feet. This way the relationship is on an honest footing. She should take care to express her interest in continuing to see him. Carmen should go on the course and be aware of any situation she feels vulnerable in.

💗 At this point Carmen should keep her itchy feet to herself. She should ask a trusted colleague to act as her chaperone on the training course so she doesn't do anything she regrets.

**Dilemma Decision:** The first choice is the least helpful choice for Carmen – and probably what she'd choose. Avoiding the training course is not good for her career but even worse for her moral. She's recognized the danger signs – having itchy feet – her first positive step. Now she needs to take another positive step. The middle choice is the most positive. Talking to Greg, honestly, is that next positive step. She would now be in a position to start understanding her own puzzle piece – understanding how her background had led her into destructive behaviour that prevented her from really connecting to a man. After that, the third step would be to identify her vulnerable moments on the course and then get out of the situation. The last choice places the onus of responsibility on a work colleague to look after her. Not good for her professional reputation, but i. good for her confidence which she needs to develop.

Carmen's a fairly typical terrorist. They usually test a man with blatantly bad behaviour – frequently involving other men. By jeopardizing their new relationship, these women prove to themselves that they're not cut out for relationships. So they go about their life managing to avoid what they fear most – intimacy. Worse, yet, sometimes this behaviour confirms their sense that they're unlovable. As this is the perspective they have of the world, having it confirmed, in the short run at least, keeps them from having to seriously evaluate how they face issues like trust and intimacy.

 ## Cheryl's Experience

Cheryl is a good example of the sorts of behaviour that would be destructive to a relationship. She wasn't really aware of her problem being evident to others until a work colleague pulled her aside and spoke to her about some behaviour she had witnessed. Before this incident, Cheryl had always had a sense that she wanted to 'upset' or 'test' the men she dated. But she didn't see herself as being transparent to others.

d been seeing someone, Jason, from the office
and had been detonating random surprises for
the first she had embarrassed him at a gather-
ends. Cheryl had gone over the top with some
risqué jokes. Some had laughed along with Cheryl, others pre-
tended not to hear the jokes. Jason was perplexed – Cheryl
never said things like that at the office!

The next time they went out Cheryl was generally being
too affectionate. Jason had drawn away a bit but she had per-
sisted. After that they met her friends in a bar for drinks. Cheryl
had started teasing him about work related things. Between
such bizarre pieces of behaviour, Cheryl seemed in tune with
Jason when they spoke at work. This discrepancy in her behaviour confused him. Were dating nerves at the bottom of it?

Confusing the enemy is one of the tactics of a terrorist. If
they confuse the man, it gives them the time to consider
whether, or not, they might dip their toe further into this particular pool of romance. As Jason thought she was great around
the office – bright and attractive – he decided to get to know
her better so that she would begin to feel confident. How was
he to know that Cheryl would continually test his patience?

The crunch for Cheryl came when the colleague noticed
her behaviour at a work event. Games were to be played and
different department heads were team captains. They paired
colleagues off for the events. As Cheryl was on a team opposite

Jason, she kept making big scenes when her team won. She acted like a child and it was all aimed in his direction. Her colleague asked her what was up – had Cheryl realized what a scene she had created?

Cheryl described her deep embarrassment that she could be so blinkered about her own behaviour. She had been so totally involved in pushing Jason's buttons and testing the depth of his interest that she'd forgot about the attention she was drawing to herself. This behaviour was also fuelling her relationship pattern. Cheryl had gone from man to man and had never managed to get off the starting block. She had a true avoidance pattern propelled along by such destructive behaviour that she didn't even get to the fling stage.

It was clear that she wasn't always predictable in the sorts of destructive behaviour she employed to avoid intimacy. Sometimes, as with Jason, she was very immature. Other times she would behave very badly with other men in front of the one who was interested in her. In fact her three dates with Jason were about as far as she'd ever got!

 ## Cheryl's Personal Enhancement Strategies

After exploring Cheryl's difficult behaviour, it was apparent she needed to learn to control impulsive behaviour generally in her life.

♥ Identify impulses – Cheryl needed to learn to identify *when* impulsive thoughts started to go through her mind. These thoughts were at the root of impulsive behaviour and needed to be prevented. Cheryl was to keep a diary and pen at hand to record these. After a week, we analysed these to see if there was an identifiable pattern. There wasn't one but she felt the use of the diary had increased her awareness of the link between an impulsive thought taking shape and the possible behaviour that arose from it.

♥ Keeping calm – with this increased self-awareness, Cheryl decided she should take up a calming pastime. She tried a yoga and meditation class. Although at first she was impatient with the techniques, after a few weeks she felt an inner calm developing.

♥ Increasing self-esteem – Cheryl needed to build up her self-esteem. This had taken a pounding with her parents' divorce. Cheryl had a few 'heart to hearts' with her mother. She needed 'closure' on a couple of issues surrounding the divorce. Had she made it worse for her parents with her demanding behaviour? Did her mother really mean all the things she'd said about her father during the divorce? Cheryl's anxieties were in part laid to rest with this new, open discussion with her mother leading to improved self-esteem.

**Cheryl's Romantic Enhancement Strategies**

Cheryl needed to learn she could treat boyfriends in the same way she treated friends. Not as the enemy, but as individuals whom needed respect just as friends do. This would also involve feeling better about herself as a romantic partner. Up until this point, Cheryl had always expected to be let down by men.

- Romantic affirmations – just before going out on a date, Cheryl was to give herself a pep talk. These would include reminding herself that taking it one step at a time would not open herself up to too much intimacy. Therefore, inner fears about intimacy would be kept in check. That she must be aware of impulsive thoughts about behaving strangely towards men. And that she could have fun without dropping bombshells along the way.

- Romantic empathy – Cheryl was to imagine the way the man felt about their date. He might be just as worried or anxious. She was to conjure up an image of her being calm and confident and understanding of his needs.

- Prevention – Cheryl was to drink conservatively when around dates as alcohol seemed to unleash the worst of her impulsive terrorist behaviour. (In fact alcohol has a lot to answer for when it comes to bad behaviour in romance!)

💜 Further affirmation – Cheryl was to do a post-date self-affirmation, telling herself she was making 'progress' and to 'keep it up!'

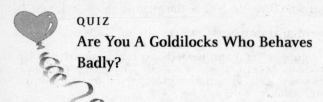

QUIZ

## Are You A Goldilocks Who Behaves Badly?

Select the answer that best describes how you feel. Then read on to find out how to handle any destructive behaviour you might have so you can reach your relationship potential!

**1 Have you ever played games or tried upsetting the man you were seeing, possibly for attention?**

A  No, there are positive ways of getting attention

B  Yes, I frequently play games or upset them to get their attention

C  I occasionally play games

**2 Have you had affairs or does the thought constantly cross your mind?**

A  No, I wouldn't have affairs

B  I've had many or have considered them many times

C  It's a possibility

**3** Do you flirt to the point you know it could cause trouble between you and your boyfriend?

  A No, I wouldn't

  B Yes, I do flirt

  C Occasional flirting is fine

**4** Would you generally describe your past relationships as:

  A Emotionally healthy?

  B Emotionally unhealthy?

  C Hard to make a generalization along those lines?

**5** Have men ever accused you of being difficult or unreasonable?

  A No

  B Yes, frequently

  C Maybe once or twice

**6** Do friends worry about the way you conduct relationships?

  A No, they don't worry

  B Yes, they worry a lot

  C They've been worried at times

**7** Do you feel scared when you get emotionally close to a man?

  A No, I don't feel scared

  B Yes, I do

  C Sometimes it's a bit scary

**8** Do you worry about being dumped – so you dump first?

   **A** No, I wouldn't behave like that

   **B** Yes, frequently

   **C** I have done that on occasion

**9** Do you always feel tempted to 'test' a man's love for you?

   **A** No, feelings aren't there to be tested

   **B** Yes, I always test the way they feel about me

   **C** Sometimes I do little tests like the 'three-day-phone-call' rule

## GOLDILOCKS KEY

Four + **Bs** and you're probably a relationship terrorist! (**B** answers to 2, 7, and 8 also add up to 'terrorism'!) You need to get to the bottom of what drives your relationship style. Right now you may enjoy the roller coaster of your romantic life but down the line you risk great unhappiness. The longer you carry on like this the harder it is to change.

### Key romantic message = Be composed before you act!

Take small steps to improve your self-confidence. If you're frightened of emotions, then you need to slowly build your ability to cope with strong ones. Don't rush things as this will bring the fear rushing on.

If you always treat men the same way, try to break this chain of behaviour. Perhaps on date number two, you always try their patience. Don't do that – make sure that date is doing something fun that won't leave you open to destructive behaviour.

If you doubt your own worth, try to highlight your good points. Focus on these and stop your thoughts roaming to your weak points. Remind yourself why you'd be a good 'catch'.

Take small steps in disclosing your personal feelings. A terrorist M.O. (*Modus Operandum*) usually involves dishonesty about her feelings. Make small disclosures about yourself, your history, and your feelings as you get to know someone.

As with negative behaviour found in any of the Goldilocks styles, take note of when you're most vulnerable to behaving badly. Perhaps it's when a man pays you a compliment or seems keen. These set alarm bells ringing in your head and you decide to test whether he really means it! Don't test, simply enjoy the moment.

If you're seeking attention with your destructive behaviour, try some positive methods for getting that attention you crave! Develop your own unique skills and talents that draw attention to you and your interests – not drive men crazy wondering what you're playing at!

Mainly **As** – you are not at risk from this destructive relation-ship style. You may fall into one of the other styles but at least you aren't dropping emotional bombs into his lap.

Mainly **Cs** – you are at risk of falling into the terrorist trap. Once you start playing around and act in questionable ways it's a slippery slope to an all out battle of the sexes.

🗝 If you enjoy taking risks, rather than take risks in your relationships, participate in some challenging activities. Take up an action sport or throw yourself into new chal-lenges at work. This should fulfil this need and leave you feeling calmer in your romantic life.

🗝 Don't get involved too quickly. Allow yourself a few dates to decide if he's worth going out with. If not break it off gently – don't push him away with unpredictable behav-iour because it's easier for you!

🗝 Check out the advice for fully-fledged terrorists and put it to use in your own life.

## Chapter Seven

# Goldilocks Style Five

## Too Much, Too Soon

I've talked earlier in this book about dipping your toe into the romantic pond. I think it's a particularly good metaphor to use to describe this Goldilocks style – 'too much, too soon'. While most of us dip our toe into that pool of romance, this sort of woman dives in headfirst. And as she plunges through the romantic waters, she bellyflops and slams head first into the bottom of the pool – ouch! She doesn't have any romantic self-control and repeatedly tends to fail in relationships.

Women with this style pursue relationships with enormous effort. They really give it their 'all'. At first look you might think, 'What a positive approach to men!' But with only a little time and consideration you'd see that actually she has all the finesse of a bull in a china shop. She crashes through relationship after relationship, expecting so much to happen from the word go. It doesn't though for many reasons. Imagine Goldilocks gobbling up all those porridges, then finding she's got a tummy ache. Or exclaiming as soon as she lies down that the bed is 'perfect' and waking with a backache.

We've all had friends who expect 'too much, too soon'. She claims to be 'in love' after the first date: 'He's so perfect!' she says. On the second she's tattooed his name on her hip (only a 'tasteful' tattoo she assures you) and by the third she's planning the wedding – only to get dropped like a lead weight as soon as he realizes that she's not joking – she does want to have his babies! Even though she hasn't even begun to get past his dating mask. He figures she must be crazy to get serious this quickly when she must know, after all, that he's still on his absolute best behaviour. 'Doesn't she want to see the real me?' he thinks.

# Typical 'Too Much, Too Soon' Behaviour

- ❤ She has heaps of praise for the new man in her life.

- ❤ She insists that she's never met anyone like him – or that he's different.

- ❤ She's blind to a new man's bad behaviour.

- ❤ She's frequently heard saying: 'I'm so in love!', 'He's the most amazing, perfect, wonderful guy!' and, 'I never thought I could feel like this again!'

- ❤ She stops ringing girlfriends because she totally focuses on him.

- ❤ She has 'romantic amnesia' about how frequently she falls in love.

- ❤ She's heavily dependent on girlfriends once it's over.

# Where Does This Style Come From?

- ❤ They might have felt abandonment in their early years – possibly through divorce and the sense of loss from that experience. Now they set about jeopardizing their relationships by demanding too much, too soon. In the long run they are, of course, going to experience loss again because they eventually push men away through their emotionally demanding style.

💗 No good role model existed within their family for constructing lasting relationships. Therefore these women don't know how to construct a positive relationship based on emotional balance. Instead they act with 'imbalance' asking for too much.

💗 They've been raised in families who act through emotion and not through thought. Everything they did became a drama and they take this style of interacting into their adult relationships expecting them to be fraught with emotion.

💗 Women may fear intimacy for one of many reasons and this style allows them to avoid intimacy by pushing men away. For example, a woman may have been heartbroken by rejection in a past romantic relationship. She never repaired this emotional damage and now although she'd love to be in a relationship, she can't actually allow herself to trust someone. So she dives in and suddenly panics giving out mixed messages.

💗 She may have been doted on as a child and quite simply expects a lot of love, very quickly.

# The Main Reasons Why This Goldilocks Style Won't Let You Reach Your Relationship Potential

❤ Men don't like feeling they're being pushed. The man runs a mile but not before she's begged, pleaded, sobbed, and sworn they can make it work so: 'Please don't go!' she cries. This behaviour makes the man back off even more quickly. He may even be tempted to change address and get an unlisted number to boot!

❤ The women, themselves, often get bored and restless after awhile – what they thought was 'it' – the one for them – actually wasn't! They tire of trying to make something they rushed into work and bow out quickly. Often they end up with little respect for the men they've badgered into a relationship – albeit a pretend one. So the women who want 'too much, too soon' realize these men can't give it to them. They constantly find misfits in their search for the right puzzle piece, which they discard.

❤ Other women who dive in like this, suddenly end up rather scared by the whole thing. 'What have I started?' they wonder as panic slowly sets in. 'Can I get out of it?' is the next question. That's when the panic takes over and they make slapdash decisions about how to squirm out of the situation. This fear often comes from a sense that either they've made themselves vulnerable (I've jumped in and he could jump out just as quickly!) or they fear the intimacy they've achieved so quickly.

 The cycle is in place. The heartbreak of being dumped, or the relief of escaping one misjudged relationship (if she's got bored or scared) gives way all too quickly to desperation to get into the next – because it *will* be the right one! Desperation impels her to grab what she can as soon as she finds it, without thinking about it! It's all emotion and *no* thought. Frequently this reflects low self-confidence. The woman believes she won't be able to keep a man if she does not rope him in quickly. She finds it impossible to pace her relationships and this stops her getting to the heart of her relationship potential.

## When This Style Might Be A Success

Of course this relationship style may work with a man who is similarly intense and impulsive. The two of you together will want 'too much, too soon' – and get it. Hopefully it works! It may also succeed with a man who's rather weak and can be pushed down the road of romance. But would you like a man like that anyway?

# Joan's Experience

Joan's case illustrates how far some women will go to rope in a man because they fear losing him right from the start. She was an extreme 'too much, too sooner' and went off her birth control pills soon after meeting Steve – without telling him! Joan decided he was *the* one – she'd never felt this way before! But she was suffering from 'romantic amnesia' because her friends had heard her say this at least half a dozen times before. Joan felt so strongly and didn't want to leave anything to chance. She'd get pregnant and get her man that way.

By the time I met her, the pregnancy plan, fortunately, had not materialized but her relationship with Steve ended fairly disastrously. She was depressed and had pretty much let herself go in an emotional sense. She felt there was no future to look forward to and her relationship potential seemed out of reach.

Joan recounted how at first, things were going well. She and Steve had become intensely involved very early. Joan admitted there had been moments Steve had questioned the intensity of their relationship. He said he'd never got so involved that quickly. Joan took this as more proof that they were 'meant' for each other.

After three intense months together Joan disclosed to Steve her hopes for falling pregnant. Steve was stunned – how could she have without consulting him? What was going through her head? Joan was sure that if she now confessed 'all', Steve would be thrilled that she had hoped to bring them together this way. True to this Goldilocks style Joan had completely misjudged his reaction. She had floated off on to a cloud of her own romantic reality that had no bearing on their shared reality! Steve broke off the relationship, suggesting she get help. Joan felt intense guilt over the break up. Now she questioned her relationship track record.

Joan wanted to move forward – she was an emotional wreck after all. But again true to the 'too much, too soon' style, she felt maybe she could simply leave this – dump it into some unknown emotional dumpster and forget it. She thought she'd get out of this malaise by cutting the memories out rather than facing the emotional issues that had driven such behaviour.

On exploring her past relationship pattern, she was a true serial flinger – quite a common pattern for women with this relationship style. Joan had previously leapt from one brief relationship to another. Usually they ended quite quickly with the men being frightened off. Joan had thought nothing of telling someone she was 'in love' by their third date. Recognizing her pattern was the first step. And now it was time to get to grips with her relationship style – the intense emotional neediness that characterized this.

##  Joan's Personal Enhancement Strategies

Joan had serious emotional exploring to do. Her PESs were going to be more intense than most. Joan's emotional neediness had roots in her childhood. She described her mother as being very distant and involved in her career. She felt she'd had a raw deal when it came to the love she craved as a child.

- Role play – we started with role play. Joan spoke to me as if I was her mother and explained her feelings of need. After a few attempts she opened up to the role play and found it enlightening. I came back to her with a number of responses to get her thinking of the possibility that she was loved more than she felt. Her mother had parented her in the only way she knew – it didn't mean she didn't love Joan. These sessions proved very helpful, allowing Joan to accept she was loved, if even in a way she hadn't realized. She saw her mother in new light – so important to gaining self-understanding.

- Recovery time – Joan accepted that her emotional neediness might not improve until she had time to recover from the broken relationship with Steve. She was going to take a break from dating. She was going to aim to strike up a friendship with a man at work. Joan understood that learning to build a friendship with a man first might allow her to develop better communication with men. Something she'd always done with emotion rather than thought.

💜 Enhancing approach – Joan faced up to the demanding way she also approached female friendships. She always expected them to be there and realized she probably didn't give much back. Particularly as her 'quick fix' emotional solutions to problems meant she wasn't very supportive to friends when they were in need. To help her further she was to approach friends with a more measured, calmer attitude. She was to stop making quick judgements.

💜 Calming moment – Joan was to spend a few minutes each day visualizing the 'new calmer Joan'. She was to call up this image if she felt she was slipping.

## 💜 Joan's Romantic Enhancement Strategies

Although Joan was having a break from men, this didn't prevent her from planning for the future.

💜 Emotional disclosure – we discussed a guide for emotional disclosures. This included the rate and the type of disclosure made. I asked Joan for a list of the things she used to talk about on the first couple of dates. I was *not* surprised to see she often discussed the inner workings of her family, her past relationships in detail, and asked quite personal questions. I then had her compile a second list containing less emotional topics – things like books, movies, holidays, and work. She understood the need for implementing the new list the next time she dated.

- Progressive work – we agreed a timetable for working up to progressively more emotional topics. This wasn't set in stone because she couldn't predict the ins and outs of how things would be with the next man in her life. However, this rough guide itself was a learning experience – something to keep her on the straight and narrow.

- Thought stopping – we worked on thought-stopping techniques. She imagined the past when she had the urge to express feelings of love. I had Joan visualize how the past men in her life might have felt and how to hold back on these verbal expressions in the future. These were to be substituted in future with expressions of 'like' or 'fondness' at the appropriate time.

- Romantic pacing – as in many of the dating styles, feeling in control of the situation gives a woman the confidence to act in a positive way. Joan was to pace carefully future romantic situations – definitely not rush into things like accepting a date straightaway. Or insisting they met 'that very evening' as she would in the past. Being in control of situations would give her the freedom from feeling she had to hang on to a new man.

- Letting negativity go – Joan needed to stop punishing herself for the fiasco with Steve. She expressed grief for the relationship and tried to move forward with her grieving process. She needed to let go of the guilt and learn from it. She would never again try to capture a man by anything other than compatibility and affection.

 Golden rule – Joan was to live by the rule: 'Don't mistake passion for love!'

Some reasons for the 'too much, too soon' style are even more complex. Take women who rush in head first knowing that most men will run a mile from their emotional demands. It actually means they won't have to get involved. It's a different way of avoiding intimacy than say the relationship terrorist of the last chapter, who throws a man off guard by behaving unexpectedly. Here the man is overwhelmed, doesn't like it, and leaves.

## Tammy's Experience

Tammy is a good example of a woman who actually avoided intimacy by demanding too much from men. At 33, she had never had a relationship last longer then a couple months. And no surprise either. Tammy spelled out her feelings to men from the word go. She lacked emotional sense and if she liked a man she was all over him. Unfortunately some took this as a green light to have casual sex and move on. As she handed it to them on a plate – so to speak – the love rats she encountered were only too happy to help themselves. This had left her ego severely bruised. She'd thought their night of passion meant something but they couldn't even return her calls!

The decent men she came across didn't use her as a one-night stand but were chased off soon enough. If they didn't return her many phone calls (and I'm talking many per day!), she'd get upset by their lack of attentiveness. It didn't take much to send her into a 'I'll-do-anything-to-show-them-how-much-I-care' mode. She'd cook for them, fuss over them, and be a slave in the bedroom. On the outside what she seemed to want in return was the same treatment.

Rows would develop where she'd accuse the man in her life that he didn't appreciate her or return the sort of feelings she had. As she got more emotionally demanding and argu-mentative, they would start to distance themselves. At some point late one night a girlfriend would get a call with Tammy in floods of tears. 'It's happened again!' she'd wail. 'Why can't I find a man who appreciates me?'

Friends were frequently surprised at how quickly she'd bounce back. When speaking to her it became apparent why. Inside she was actually relieved in a funny sort of way. Tammy couldn't really face a serious relationship. She felt she didn't have the emotional 'know how' to deal with men at an intimate level. Tammy simply didn't understand them and it seemed she'd never reach her relationship potential.

Having grown up with two sisters, men were quite a mystery. There had also been a tension between the sisters in the form of competition for each other's boyfriends. Tammy had always felt insecure as a result – she wasn't as outgoing as her sisters or as successful at the romance game. This early tension in the dating arena had left her quite insecure. She felt the pressure to be with someone – or else be the odd one out who didn't have a boyfriend.

Her style made it easy to say she was involved – she could talk about her present boyfriend – but deep inside she feared it. Diving in at the deep end had rescued her from daring to have a relationship – because it all ended so quickly. It also gave her some kudos in an odd sort of way to have had so many boyfriends. We identified Tammy's pattern as usually a serial flinger but at times an erratic. Tammy was surprised herself to look at her relationships, as a first step, in this way. This first piece of her relationship puzzle helped confirm to her that things needed to change.

 **Tammy's Dilemma**

Tammy has been told by one of her sisters that one of Tammy's recent 'exs' – Joe – wants to have another chance. Her sister, Jane, was talking to Joe because she likes him now. Joe said that maybe Tammy *is* the one for him and wishes he hadn't finished it so quickly when things got heavy. Tammy feels uncomfortable about Jane admitting she likes Joe. There were a few options open to Tammy. If you've been one to expect 'too much, too soon', then you'll probably recognize how you might normally respond.

❤ Tammy should definitely get back with Joe even if Jane likes him now. This may give her the chance to have her first real relationship. And she was the one who originally went out with Joe so Jane will have to accept this. If it doesn't work, it doesn't work!

❤ Tammy should not go back to Joe as it will be too complicated with Jane's feelings to consider. She should really look elsewhere. If Jane ends up going out with Joe, then she'll have to accept that.

❤ Tammy should not go back to Joe because right now she needs to get on an even keel. She should be open with Jane about the emotional turmoil she's been in recently. This honestly may be rewarded with consideration rather than 'games' – the way the sisters have often treated each other.

**Dilemma Decision:** If you've got a tendency towards diving in head first, you probably were tempted to choose the first – and allow Tammy to throw herself back into the romantic fray! Tammy needs a period of emotional stability – as is the case with so many women who experience relationship difficulties – whatever their style. Returning to an 'ex' with the great possibility of failing again, as well as worrying about her sister's feelings, would not be helpful. The most helpful choice would be the last. Tammy needs to be honest with those in her life that affect her relationships. And both her sisters have affected her outlook. Honesty now will have a positive affect on her outlook. The middle option does not allow for the emotional breather she now needs.

QUIZ
## Are You A Goldilocks Who Dives In Head First?

Now it's time to look at just how far you might fit into this Goldilocks style. If you acknowledge honestly the way you'd normally respond to the following questions, this should give you a good guide as to how much you need to slow down.

**1 Inside do you feel you really need a man in your life?**

A  Yes, because I think it's important to share your life with a partner

B  Yes, because I can't stand the thought of being on my own

C  Yes, because I feel the pressure to settle down

**2 Someone at work has been giving you the eye:**

A  I'd have to carefully consider what the repercussions of taking it further might be

**B** At the next opportunity I'd flirt with him to see what he's like

**C** I'd ask around to find out more about him

**3** **Do you rush into things that you end up regretting – like volunteering to take on some responsibility you really don't want?**

**A** No, I'm careful what I do with my time

**B** Yes, many times I've ended up doing things I really didn't want to

**C** There have been times I've regretted taking things on

**4** **How often do you get the feeling that men are wary of you?**

**A** I've never really had that feeling

**B** I've often felt they're wary of me, and so I have to prove myself

**C** From time to time I've been aware that they're trying to second guess me

**5** **Have you felt the same way about many men that you've been in love with?**

**A** No, when I've been in love it's always been for unique reasons

**B** Yes, I've felt the same passion for many men

**C** Sometimes I get a sense of *deja vu* in my feelings

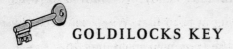

# GOLDILOCKS KEY

Three+ **Bs** – you probably go for 'too much, too soon'.

Three+ **Cs** – you might end up expecting 'too much, too soon'.

Three+ **As** – you don't dive in head first.

Try these to stop yourself diving in head first:

## Key romantic message = Take time to be sure!

Where does this need come from? Is there an area of your emotional life you could re-evaluate, accept, and move on as Joan did with her feelings about her mother.

Watch out when you're feeling vulnerable for whatever reason. It could be your boss has upset you or you've argued with your best friend. This is when you'll want to dive in for some emotional comfort from a man. It won't be much comfort when he runs a mile!

Again, control is an important issue – you need to regulate your impulsive emotions. When you start bandying about the word 'love' – stop and re-evaluate the budding romance. How can you love someone you've only spent two evenings with? You may think he's intelligent, funny, and sexy – but love him? No!

🔑 Get a friend to be a 'crisis buddy'. Ask them to help you keep from plunging in head first. When you excitedly phone them about the new man you've met, they should talk you down a bit. Better than crying on their shoulder in three weeks time!

🔑 As with Joan, learn to slow down on the emotional disclosures. If you're tempted to turn the conversation to their view of marriage on the third date – don't!

🔑 Until you're confident about keeping this tendency in control, let the man take the romantic lead. Not something I recommend that often! Most men are quite frankly slower about professing love, getting obsessed with us, and letting go – so let him do it first. And hopefully you'll learn to reach your relationship potential!

Chapter Eight

# Goldilocks Style Six

## Too Little, Too Late

Just as some women give 'too much, too soon', so too do many women give 'too little, too late'. We've all had friends who make us pull our hair out. We watch with horror as they lose a great guy simply because they have the capacity to show as much emotion as an iceberg. Usually through fear or anxiety these women hold back from demonstrating real love within relationships. For most women, getting involved with a man involves emotional disclosure. This disclosure takes place over a number of weeks or months as they slowly build trust, and certainty, in the importance of the relationship. Step by step, they allow the new man in their life to glimpse their 'real' self. Their dating mask slips but only as and when they want it to. Men, in a different way, as we shall see in coming chapters, also undergo stages of disclosure. However, the woman who has a 'too little, too late' relationship style never manages to work through the stages of emotional disclosure towards intimacy.

 # The Main Stages Of Emotional Disclosure

Now is a good point to look at this large piece of the relationship puzzle: the stages of emotional disclosure. There are five main stages I like to work with. Negotiating these successfully will help your relationship.

1. **Mystery** – the chemical reaction stage! Oh, those early days fuelled by chemistry but also dogged by mystery. The high you're on is tempered by your doubt surrounding his level of interest. During the mystery phase you uncover the non-threatening demographics: 1. Getting to know the basics of each other's work life: how hard you work, what level of priority work takes in the overall structure of your life, etc. 2. What your interests are – and whether they're compatible. For example, does one of you like to go out drinking in bars all night while the other is a health nut? (Might not

make it past the mystery stage in this case!) 3. The basics of family background. But *not* the intimacies like how your father ran off with his secretary or his brother is a ne'er-do-well! 4. And the overall shape your life tends to take. Is it hugely busy and fast paced, or is it calm and laid back? Flirting goes on but it's still a complete mystery where this new thing will go. You're very much on guard with full dating mask on. The 'too little, too late' woman will keep it firmly in place.

**Recognition** – you can now anticipate when his next phone call will be – you're beginning to know him! The caginess surrounding what you tell him is beginning to go. You're beginning to meet each other's friends. You recognize that a relationship might be developing. Disclosures now take the form of hinting at your feelings and giving more away about the various aspects of your life. You may disclose things about work-related dreams, or a life-long passion (wanting to write romantic poetry!), that you may have felt foolish talking about earlier on.

**Plateau** – the toothbrush stage – by now you've moved yours over to his house! You now actually manage to get some sleep when you two spend the night together. This is the stage many relationships don't survive. Irritating habits can become more noticeable as you spend more time together. You may also start to introduce each other to family.

**4** **Adaptation** – the mask has nearly slipped! You can pretty much be yourself but there are still times you think better of it! You are both (hopefully) adapting to and accommodating each other's ways. This is the real stage of compromise. If you can't compromise now, you won't survive. Disclosures are now quite intimate. Trust has been built so you don't expect him to laugh when you tell him your deepest fears – like making strange noises during lovemaking!

**5** **Intimacy** – you bare all! You now allow him to see you when you're ill, without make-up, or in your worst moods. But this can be a wonderful time for you two. You know and love each other. You have someone to share the good and bad with. It can become so strong and committed that it feels like it's you two against the world.

The woman with this Goldilocks style usually remains fixed in the 'mystery phase' – even if she appears to be getting deeper into a romance. A 'too little, too late' woman is very good at camouflaging the fact that she is simply going through the motions. On the surface things seem to be moving along. But inside, usually she knows she's not being 'herself' to the man. I say 'usually' because sometimes a woman doesn't realize she's not letting herself go emotionally. She has become so detached from her real feelings that although she knows she's not happy in a relationship, or it doesn't feel right, she can't put her finger on why.

Think of a Goldilocks who plays with her food! She moves from bowl to bowl simply swirling the spoon around, making it look as if she's tasted it but in reality she's simply dipped her spoon in and messed about. Then she might go from bed to bed simply ruffling the covers a bit, but not actually lying down. People might not guess that she hasn't actually given it a shot. But she never reaches her relationship potential.

In terms of the relationship pattern it seems to be there – this style doesn't necessarily mean these women will have the avoidance pattern. They date in one form or another – but the style is one of emotional distance that is well hidden at least for a time.

Usually when thinking of someone who withholds from a relationship, we conjure up an image of an ice maiden in the bedroom – a woman who won't let go in her sexual relationship. This may also be true of a woman who gives 'too little, too late' emotionally. As well as having difficulties with emotional commitment, she may also find it hard to let go in bed. Some women sexually 'act out', though. They're tigresses in the bedroom simply because they crave human contact but can't get it emotionally.

# Typical 'Too Little, Too Late' Behaviour

💜 She learns to play the relationship game with finesse at least on the outside. But friends will notice her self-doubts and game playing.

💜 She may be guilty of appearing two-faced. Saying one thing to the man in her life and the opposite to friends.

💜 She may tease and joke too much as a way of deflecting attention from herself.

💜 She says things like: 'It's going great but he seems to want to know everything about me!' Even if the poor guy simply wants to know the usual stuff she feels threatened by it.

💜 When it ends in tears, she's likely to blame it on the man: 'He didn't understand me!' The second most likely reason is: 'He didn't give me enough space!'

# Where Does This Style Come From?

💜 Fear and anxiety is at the root of this style. But unlike the 'too much, too soon' style, it drives these women away from men rather than rushing towards them.

- A distant, unloving family background where a tight lid is kept on emotions is likely to be behind this style. The woman grows up expecting emotional distance and is wary of anything else.

- Or it may arise from an emotional trauma. Such women then decide that giving love and showing emotions is too painful. They start to deny their feelings and are very detached in their relationships.

 # The Main Reasons Why This Goldilocks Style Prevents You Reaching Your Relationship Potential

- Because these women miss out on men who want a caring relationship. Many men have intuition, too! They can sense when someone's really not involved.

- This style leads to disappointment in themselves, as deep down they long for true intimacy and they know they are failing to allow this.

- It also leads to disappointment in the men they try to fit into their style. They may choose men who are also emotionally detached. Or men who are good at sensing a woman with deep vulnerability and take advantage of this. And these women are deeply vulnerable in reality.

## When This Style Might Be A Success

A woman who withholds her love may actually find success in relationships with certain types of men. Picture the sort of couple who are both very busy. They have their own interests, friends, or work long hours, and don't live in each other's pockets – at all! It is quite possible to function in this sort of relationship as a Goldilocks who withholds her emotions and never crosses into intimate territory. This may suit you and it may suit him.

It may also succeed with a man who is determined to change you. Some men are driven to change the women in their lives (just as *most* women fall into the trap of trying to change their men – to mould that puzzle piece to an acceptable shape). This style is very challenging to these men. They are drawn to women who give little and can be persistent in their attempts to change that. You and he end up in a stand-off that might work. But who wants that?

 ## Charlotte's Experience

When I met Charlotte, I was struck by her quiet intelligence and soft-spoken voice. When the topic turned to relationships, another side to her became apparent. At 28, she'd had three long relationships, each lasting about two years. Charlotte was a true serial monogamist without ever having reached emotional depth in any of these.

Her last partner, Simon, had finished the relationship with anger and recrimination. After giving all, he felt Charlotte had simply lapped it up, never giving in return. And Simon was right. Charlotte described never feeling able to be her 'real' self in a relationship. By 'real' self she said others saw her as intelligent and sensible but didn't realize how confused she was inside.

Marital breakdown was the norm in Charlotte's family. Her father was on wife number three and her mother had just divorced Charlotte's step-father. She described both her parents as 'difficult' – emotionally demanding but never giving. Two 'too little, too late' types who had met and married. They coasted through marriage with their own emotions on hold. Quite an unsatisfactory combination!

Charlotte had never really learned how to connect with others at a deep level. She'd also been quite scarred by her parents' behaviour. No wonder she was confused about relationships. Until now, she thought if she stayed cool and calm it would work. But actually she erected barriers between her real emotions and what she showed to men. She knew she'd had a good man in Simon and wondered if she could change enough to win him back.

##  Charlotte's Dilemma

Simon had left the relationship with so much frustration that Charlotte was frightened of asking him to think about reconciling. If you tend to hold back in love, you may recognize the option she first chose:

- ❤ Charlotte should confess her fears over intimacy to Simon honestly and ask him to consider trying again.

- ❤ Charlotte should stand back from her desire to put things right with Simon and instead try to find intimacy in her next relationship.

- ❤ Charlotte should not confess her fears to Simon but instead ask to build a friendship if he's willing and then take it from there.

**Dilemma Decision:** If you chose the second option that was the one Charlotte initially suggested. And it's not the best option. It allows her once again 'to put her emotions off' – this time to the next relationship. Of course she shouldn't expect that Simon would even be interested in a second chance. So she might have to stand back. But instead she should be prepared to tell all to Simon. And then let him decide if he's prepared to give it a second chance. The reason being is that she essentially deceived him at an emotional level. Whereas he was getting involved slowly but surely, she never let herself go and certainly never confided in him. She has amends to make.

It's a good starting point to 'come out' to him, even if it only cleans the slate. But it does allow her to explore her emotions with someone who may then help her to work through her fears. Selecting the last option is still operating in a 'half-way house' as far as her opening up about emotions is concerned.

It's difficult to change from this Goldilocks style. It cocoons you from possible hurt but damages your ability to relate. Often the latter seems the lesser of the two evils. But if you want to reach your relationship potential, you need to change this major piece of the relationship puzzle by putting your emotions on the line.

 **Gemma's Experience**

Gemma was 38 when she decided she wanted her next relationship to be a real one. She'd always felt she was acting a part in the past. Part of the impetus was losing her mother to cancer. Gemma felt a terrible void in her life. She'd been close to her mother and longed for another close relationship. She knew she couldn't replace her mother with a man but Gemma felt ready to commit to something lasting. These thoughts made her uneasy – how could she let go?

Gemma had finished a relationship with Anthony, which had lasted nearly a year. As the relationship grew, she found herself growing angrier with him. The slightest transgression and she would snap. Poor Anthony didn't know if he was coming or going. Gemma described such frustration that at the end, she could barely stand to look at him. But inside she was angry with herself! Whereas Anthony made genuine efforts to get close, she would get more annoyed. Inside she envied his ability to trust. She also got angry with him: 'Can't he guess that I'm not really trying here?' she'd think. It's as if she expected him to mind read, and then to coax her into giving more.

Gemma had many unhappy relationships. On the outside they looked different but they were linked with one common strand – her play-acting. Gemma really couldn't understand where this came from. Exploring her family relationships led to more insight. She was the 'baby' of four children and had two brothers and one sister. She felt pretty spoiled by the amount of attention she'd received. Everyone doted on the 'baby' – particularly as there was a large gap before she arrived.

When Gemma got out into the real world, though, she was no longer the centre of attention. This shook her confidence. Before she'd basked in the family limelight – now she was one of many players in the game of life. In the past, her mother always made a fuss over her.

So how did this transfer to her relationships? Gemma would try and judge how best to act to become the centre of a man's world. She'd play a part. If he was a quiet, thoughtful man, she'd put on a 'book wormish' personality. If he was sports mad and loud, she'd throw herself into extrovert behaviour. Over time she tired of her roles. Either the man would see through her – and dump her because she was phoney. Or she'd get angry with the situation and dump him. Her pattern veered from serial flings to serial monogamy, depending on how long it took either of them to see she wasn't genuine.

 **Gemma's Personal Enhancement Strategies**

Gemma needed some PESs to help her be herself and appreciate and develop her real emotions. This would help free her from the 'too little, too late' style and let her reach her relationship potential.

- Giving attention – Gemma needed to feel at ease with sharing the limelight. She was to actively encourage friends to shine. One friend, who was shy, responded positively to Gemma helping her place some phone calls in looking for a new job. Simple things like this had Gemma feeling good about how others' needs could be met. And by giving something of herself, it was a big step to learning to give to relationships – even her friendships had been marred by her lack of emotional commitment.

- Being valued – Gemma needed to learn that being the centre of attention didn't necessarily mean being valued more. Attention was a roving spotlight – it landed on you sometimes. And not at others. Gemma was to accept attention happily when it was given. And when she felt 'needy' and it wasn't forthcoming, she was to remind herself of the sorts of things that made her feel good about herself. These were to be replayed and visualized in her mind helping her to allay self-doubt.

- Writing analysis – Gemma loved writing, so some PESs aimed at self-analysis seemed appropriate. She was to write a letter to an imaginary man describing herself as she was as if they were pen pals who'd never met. Gemma then wrote a letter as if it was from him. In it he responded positively to all she'd written. Gemma was to conjure up how positive it could be to share her 'real' self. Believing is half the battle!

- Acknowledging achievement – at work Gemma was to ensure achievements didn't go unnoticed. There is nothing wrong with drawing a boss's attention to a job well done!

- Connecting to a significant other – Gemma missed her mother terribly and she decided to do something special for her. She would do things her mother had always wanted to but never got around to – like visiting Paris. Gemma made a long-term plan to save money to make this trip.

This, amongst many small things, would give her a positive sense of connection to memories of her mother.

## ❤ Gemma's Romantic Enhancement Strategies

Gemma needed to prepare for future relationships. Being able to open up emotionally was her future goal and so we planned strategies to help her now.

- ❤ Awareness of old ways – in talking to men at work, Gemma was to be aware of any play-acting she got involved in. At all times she was to be herself.

- ❤ Finding balance – as with any style where you find yourself out of balance veering to one extreme or another, practising an even-handed approach is important. Once again when chatting to men, she was to voice her ideas and thoughts – and listen to theirs. Analysing how people could have differences, but accept these as the rich tapestry of life.

- ❤ Disclosure – we worked out a plan for appropriate emotional disclosure for the future. Gemma studied the five stages of disclosure and decided she got stuck at the second – 'recognition'. She could guess what their next move would be but camouflaged her own. Drawing from past relationships, Gemma wrote up lists for each stage. How far the men had got and what they were disclosing. How comfortable, or not, she felt with these different men at the time, and what her ideal, or real, response could have been. This detailed exploration helped her recognize the sorts of barriers she'd been erecting.

♥ Visualization – I asked Gemma to visualize her romantic aura. This aura is like a perfume she'd wear – the vibe she'd like to give off to men in the future and how this encapsulated the real her. It took a lot of thought but she described her aura as sensual and quite serious, with occasional outbursts of fun. This was the real Gemma. She was quite serious, she was quite sensual, but she also liked some spontaneity in her life. She was going to bring this aura to her next relationship.

♥ Moving forward – Gemma agreed that when next attracted to a man she was not going to play-act to fit in with him. Instead she was going to be herself. She accepted if the attraction was there, it wasn't necessarily due to them being the same – it could be their differences!

Gemma now accepted she needed to stop withholding if relationships were to succeed. She'd lost some of the fear of being herself. And now this big piece of her relationship puzzle was in place – she'd no longer conceal her 'real' self or give 'too little, too late'.

## QUIZ
## Are You A Goldilocks Who Gives 'Too Little, Too Late'?

Are you jeopardizing relationships by putting up barriers to your emotions? And then withholding from committing to the men in your life? Think through these scenarios and find out whether you have the tendency to withhold.

**1 You've been dating a man for four weeks. It's obvious he's getting more emotionally involved than you are. You aren't quite sure of your feelings yet. Which would you be most likely to do?**

**A** His feelings are his responsibility. I can't change that. I might carry on seeing how my feelings develop before saying anything to him.

**B** I'd let him know that I wasn't sure of my feelings yet. But I'd be positive and ask him for more time to work them out.

**C** This would frighten me, if he felt more deeply than I did. It might make me back off.

**2 A new man starts working in the suite of offices next to yours. You find him very attractive and interesting looking. How would you get his attention?**

**A** I'd ask him if he needed any help finding things in the local area. This would be a good way to start talking about work that might lead on to other topics.

**B** I'd wait to see if he made a move to talk to me. I wouldn't want to embarrass myself by being obvious when I have to work next door to him.

**C** I'd find out through co-workers what they knew about him, like: 'What does he do?' And 'Is he free?' Then I might try and get his attention without appearing interested.

**3** **You want to end a relationship. You have your reasons but you've never discussed them with him. How would you handle this?**

**A** I'd probably push him away slowly at an emotional level. It's hard to face talking about breaking up.

**B** I'd let him down gently. There's no point in going into the gory details of why I'm unhappy. I don't want to upset him.

**C** I'd feel it's best to talk about what's not working. Who knows – maybe it could be sorted out? If not, at least I'd walk away with a clean slate.

# GOLDILOCKS KEY

**1–C, 2–B, 3–A:** You give 'too little, too late'! How to reach your relationship potential:

## Key Romantic Message = It's time to let go and live a little!

- Identify your anxiety – why do you withhold? Was emotional disclosure a 'no-no' in your family? Or has a bad experience made you wary? It's time to let go of the past and take some romantic risks!

- Practise visualizing how you'd like to be! Would you rather be more confident in your choices? Or more sure of your own emotions? Imagine everyday, in your mind's eye, working to this goal. You can begin to trust yourself.

- Identify where you get to in the five stages of disclosure. Next time the romantic cards are on the table allow yourself to go to the next stage.

- Just as with women who give 'too much, too soon', you may need to go with the flow the man provides. Listen to him. If he's disclosing a bit about his childhood take this as your cue to do so. Eventually you'll feel good enough to simply let down the barriers in a natural way that suits you.

- Try some honesty. If it's very hard to let go, and you're worried you'll lose a great guy, tell him that you've got a bit of a struggle to get through. If he's worth it, he'll be patient.

🗝 Don't choose men who appear distant – I'm sure you'll recognize them. This will throw you back into your old ways. It'll become a power struggle both of you will want to win – but you'll both lose.

🗝 Think of the biggest part of your puzzle – the qualities you have to offer that you've been withholding. What sort of qualities do you think would complement yours? Think of the men you've felt most comfortable with in the past (and that you've not given to!) – this may lead you to who might suit you in the future.

1–A, 2–C, 3–B: You may be vulnerable to withholding from men.

🗝 At times you may withhold. Sometimes this is appropriate. But gauge whether or not it's justified in the circumstances. If he's let you down, seems cagey about talking about himself, or has been through lots of women, you'll be justified. Otherwise be open to getting involved.

🗝 Identify when you may get anxious over men (maybe during stage three of emotional disclosure). Watch out for these moments and act from the heart.

🗝 Use the advice above to improve your outlook to men.

**1–B, 2–A, 3–C:** You will give as much as you take! You don't withhold and are prepared to give your fair share.

Now you should be well on your way to recognizing which Goldilocks style best characterizes you! This is a big piece in your own unique relationship puzzle. Understanding how you act towards men will help you decide what might need changing. Recognition is the first piece, acting on this the next. You can do it! You may just need a bit more flexibility in your style or to cast it off completely in order to have romantic success. You've read the case histories, seen what other women have done to change, and answered the quizzes and dilemmas – all this should help you decide what to try. Now it's time to look at men – that great, unknown quantity! And try to understand them better.

Before We Move On To Part II – *Understanding Men* Memorize This:

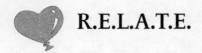

# R.E.L.A.T.E.

**R – RECOGNITION!** Learn to recognize your relationship pattern and style. They may be holding you back – and you can change them.

**E – EXPECTATIONS!** Think through your expectations. The classic Goldilocks simply expected to do a bit of testing to find the comfort she wanted. It takes a lot more self-understanding than that. Explore your expectations – are they reasonable?

**L – LOVE!** Love is a wonderful thing never to be underestimated. But make sure you love yourself first before looking for romance. You will bring the best possible you to a relationship, if you care about yourself.

**A – ATTITUDE!** The more positive your attitude, the more relationship success you'll have. Don't go in with a scared, defensive, or needy attitude – believe it or not, men can read these signs. And they will respond negatively.

**T – TOGETHER!** Togetherness is great but never lose yourself in a relationship. Two *cannot* become one and they shouldn't. Instead concentrate on the complementary sides of your puzzle pieces sitting together nicely.

**E – ENERGY!** It takes lots of energy to make a relationship work – they just don't happen.

# Part Two

# Understanding

# Him

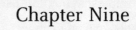

Chapter Nine

# Understanding The Way Men Think

It's time to move on to those interesting creatures – men! Many women successfully learn to understand themselves. The pieces of *their* relationship puzzle fall into place. They start to recognize their pattern – for example, they are serial monogamists. They start to recognize their style – for example, they are relationship control freaks needing everything to be done their way. And it falls into place where these come from, what it is in their family background, or experience of relationships that drives them to behave this way. But even women with this much understanding can falter at relationship hurdles because they don't go on to understand the men they meet. And understanding comes at many levels – the way men think, feel, are sexual, are romantic, and face 'commitment' in relationships. In this chapter, we are tackling the way men think.

 # The Egocentric Way We Think

Why is it that we might fail to go on to understanding men? Because we are all guilty of being egocentric, particularly when it comes to the way we think about intimate relationships! What do I mean by egocentric? That our way is the right way. That our view of the world is the correct view. Every one of you can hold your hand up and admit: 'Yes, it's hard to imagine what others think – particularly men. And I've always assumed that what I'm thinking is the most relevant thing in life.'

Of course what you think is the most relevant to *you*. But when you start interacting with another – when you want to get romantic – understanding how they think will help you reach your relationship potential. Let me give you a very common example, when you give your telephone number to a man and he says, 'I'll call soon.' You walk off thinking things like, 'I wonder when he'll call? I hope he means soon!' and, 'Will he be easy to talk to when he calls?' or panic stricken, 'What if he doesn't call? Maybe I should have taken his number!' Your initial thought sets off a chain reaction. You, as a woman, think through all the potential scenarios and possibilities that could occur over the next few days in terms of him phoning you.

And what does he think as he strides off into the sunset? Probably something like, 'She's nice – I must stick this number in my book before I lose this bit of paper. I wonder if the guys have left for football practice, yet?' Yes! That's probably the extent of his thinking processes about having your phone number – until he needs to use it! And this brings us back to a crucial point I made at the beginning of *You & Him*: men simply don't think the way we do. We often like to create imaginary scenarios of what we *think* they're thinking, but these are truly imaginary. Most men, and I stress most because there are some exceptions, do not go over every detail of a conversation, think through every eventuality, or start imagining the sorts of possibilities we women do. The exceptions are those men who are often said to be in touch with their 'feminine side'. They are the ones we like to have as friends because we can understand their thinking. They like to talk through the ins and outs of the twists and turns of their relationships.

# Why Do We Think Differently?

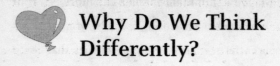

You might think it would be easier if our brains had been pro-grammed the same way – wouldn't evolution have saved a lot of hassle? All those arguments, broken relationships, and heartache, would disappear with a snap of a finger because we could understand the way the other thought. But we only need to look at our ancient ancestors to see how men and women evolved differently, largely due to our biological functions. Yes, it's true we women were constructed to give birth and then nurture the demanding little creatures – not men – babies! And rather than having men sit by, watch us 'mother' and be totally useless, they were constructed to go out and provide for us while we were temporarily restricted by our mothering role. This is not to oversimplify ancient societies because even they were complex considering the conditions that existed. And this of course does *not* mean that now, in our modern lives, we should be living like Neanderthals! With the choices many of us have, we live our lives the way we want to – children, or not, careers, or not, relationships, or not. That's the way it should be. But understanding the other's thinking will improve these choices.

We can't escape the fact, though, that deep in our ancient ancestors, the seeds were planted for the way we think now. Evolution is a very slow process. Ancient women used to have to think through how best to meet the needs of their infants, their homes, and those men when they came back from hunting. We evolved as what I call 'pre-planners' – planning for every eventuality but still from our perspective. Ancient men, on the other hand, often had to react quickly to changing weather conditions, or changing migration habits of edible animals, because capture and slaughter were all important. The target was brought down and brought home. A direct approach, 'cutting to the chase', worked best for the demands they had to meet. And a direct approach meant direct planning, extraneous thoughts were simply an interference to the task at hand.

And that brings us to modern thinking. The echoes of the past still influence the way we think. Understanding that most men have a far more direct style of thinking provides another piece of the relationship style. Accepting this difference means you can get on and work with it! Your complementary ways of thinking can actually enliven your relationship.

## Typical Examples Of How Men And Women Think *Early* In Relationships

| Topic | Men's Thoughts | Women's Thoughts |
|---|---|---|
| First dates | 'Got to have one if we're going to get anywhere!' | 'What should I wear? What's he really like? God, I look awful tonight!' |

| Attraction | 'She looks a bit like Julia Roberts.' | 'He's really good - looking – when he smiles. It's his laugh I love, though.' |
| --- | --- | --- |
| Self-image | 'I think I'm quite a good catch.' | 'I wonder if his "ex" was more fun? I can't cope with getting dumped again! Am I ready for a man?' |
| Does he/she like me? | 'I'll find out soon enough.' | 'It's hard to tell – he kept grinning. Was it nerves? Or was he happy to be out with me?' |
| What to wear? | 'This'll do.' | 'I can't wear *this* – he'll get the wrong message!' |
| What to talk about? | 'I'll ask her about her work.' | 'He'll think I'm too driven if I talk about work. Too personal, if I ask about his family.' |

**Total number of thoughts = 6 (men) versus 14 (women)**

**Type of thoughts = 'Cut to the chase' (men) versus 'pre-planning for eventualities' (women)**

Imagine these differences at work in every aspect of your fledgling relationship! And even as you get over those first hurdles and come to know each other more, if your different types of thinking aren't recognized they're bound to lead to misunderstandings! These examples illustrate that neither type is better than the other. However, it doesn't take much imagination to see that when such thoughts are verbalized many women fall into the trap of believing men are less committed to the 'cause' of their relationship. 'If he's not considering various possibilities then he's not putting as much thought into it!' I hear constantly. But no, that's not true. Men simply invest a different type of thinking into much of relationships but it doesn't mean it doesn't hold as much *meaning* for them.

An important point to note, though, is that I believe many men do more 'pre-planning' thinking than they realize or admit! When it comes to 'self-report' (telling people what they're thinking), they select out their primary thought and verbalize it. They may well have mulled over other possibilities but they quickly phase those out and stick with a thought they feel comfortable with. This is particularly true with first impressions. We all play the game – putting our best romantic foot forward – and it's hard to know just how much of the genuine article you're getting! Behind those glittering first impressions, he's probably got one primary thought: 'I've got this sorted!' and then goes on to enjoy the evening. *You*, on the other hand, have probably got a mind that won't stop ticking over thinking of every possible outcome!

 # John's And Babs' Experience

John and Babs met through work. She was immediately attracted to his go-getting nature. She'd always liked strong, motivated men. Babs also admired the clarity of his life – she tended to get bogged down with things whereas his life seemed straightforward. John found Babs fun and lively and tended to ignore the disordered side of her life. When I met them, though, it became all too clear that having a 'mutual admiration society', as they had, did *not* equal true romantic connection!

Babs had a true serial fling relationship pattern and had been pleasantly surprised to find that she was attracted enough to John to want to hang in there. But she'd also in the past tended towards a controlling relationship style. What she couldn't control, she'd discard – hence the fling pattern. And why she never got to the heart of her relationship potential. Now Babs wanted to control John's thinking, or at least be party to it!

Although Babs said how much she admired where John had got to in life, she was increasingly frustrated at what she saw as being frozen out of the detail of his life. 'I simply don't understand his way of thinking!' she moaned. John complained that

Babs nagged him for detail that wasn't important or relevant. 'Why does she want to know everything I'm thinking?' he groaned. 'We're together, we have a good life – isn't that enough?'

Clearly I had before me two people who wanted the same goal – a strong relationship – but had very different thoughts about how they should reach that goal. Because they thought differently! John and Babs needed to come to an understanding so that their relationship could work.

## 💜 John's and Babs' Relationship Enhancement Strategies

💜 Identifying each other's thinking style – John and Babs started from square one selecting a recent example of when they argued about going out. Each was to identify the train of thoughts going through their minds at the time. These were written down. They began with the initial topic, arranging a night out, and wrote down their first thought. John's = 'I've had a busy week – let's keep it simple.' Babs's = 'I'm dying to try that new restaurant. It would be wonderful to go – it's supposed to be so romantic!' Already their thoughts are starting to drift in different directions! Babs wants something 'romantic', John something 'easy'. How had their conversation progressed?

John: 'Why can't we go to our regular? It's so relaxing.'

Babs: 'Why can't we try the new place, it's supposed to be great! You're always going to great places with clients! Why can't we do something special?'

From this point their internal dialogues diverged completely. Babs couldn't understand his lack of enthusiasm. John her need for somewhere new when quite simply being together was the point of an evening out. Working through this exercise gave them immediate clarity.

### 💗 Learning to label what is meaningful

Typically a couple's divergent thinking will lead to anger on the man's part and hurt feelings on the woman's. Both John and Babs had to learn to identify what was at the heart of the other's thoughts. What was meaningful to them in terms of the topic/issue under discussion? This would help cut to the heart of the matter. So in the example above, John would identify 'relaxation' as being meaningful to him at that time. Babs would identify 'romance'. Learning to clearly state the meaning behind your thinking and conversation will reduce misunderstandings. At the outset of discussions John and Babs were each to label the meaning behind their thinking. This way from the moment a discussion got underway, they clarified their goals, which were often the same or similar!

# Learning To Accept The Way The Other Thinks

It's an important step to learn that a difference in what is being thought does not have to become a battle of one way being 'right' and one being 'wrong'. The end result should be a better understanding. Frequently this comes from understanding the thinking behind a stance that has been expressed. For example, simply because a man hasn't 'pre-planned' for every eventuality (in the thinking behind his stance), it doesn't mean that this sort of thinking on a woman's part ends in a better result. And also, even if a man has run through a number of thoughts over one issue but then expresses these thoughts in a verbally simple way like: 'Let's go somewhere relaxing,' it also doesn't mean a woman's way of expressing herself is better. Quite simply it is being prepared to recognize the differences between yourselves, and respect your different ways of thinking, which will result in compromise that enhances your romantic relationship. John and Babs worked on appreciating the other's way of thinking. They actually treated it as getting to another level of intimacy. It allowed them to talk more deeply about their thoughts on many issues without it ending in a battle of wills.

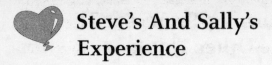

# Steve's And Sally's Experience

Now Sally and Steve seemed to be experiencing more complex problems than Babs and John. However, it became clear on exploring their relationship that they were suffering from the same sorts of difficulties. Sally felt 'neglected' because their different way of thinking about their relationship had become a barrier to their happiness. Neglect she had felt before in her relationship style where she'd tried to recreate her parents' relationship. They communicated well, which she quite understandably wanted too!

They had been married for just over a year when things really started deteriorating. Sally had begun to play a game of second-guessing what Steve was thinking. And guess why she did this? Because she couldn't believe his thinking could be so straightforward! Yes, Sally had fallen into a trap many women do as I mentioned in the introductory chapter. This trap being: to be 'mystified' by the apparent simplicity with which most men seem to think.

When Sally and Steve would discuss an issue, like whose family to visit the next free weekend they had, Sally could not accept at face value what Steve would say. So if he suggested seeing her family, Sally would immediately second-guess him. 'So are you trying to score points with my family because you're not going to be there at Christmas?' or something like that. Steve would get annoyed. Sally would then jump to the conclusion that she'd been right about what he was really thinking! Of course all along Steve did *not* have ulterior motives for most of his decisions or choices. But Sally couldn't believe it because she didn't think that way! And this was at the root of their increasingly angry disagreements stopping them reaching their relationship potential.

## 💜 Sally's and Steve's Relationship Enhancement Strategies

💜 Communicative compromises – Sally needed to help prevent arguments by stifling her habit of second-guessing. Steve needed to be a bit more explicit when discussing issues/making decisions – not explain himself but simply qualify statements. So taking the weekend example, Steve could say something like: 'Let's go to your family because I find it more relaxing. There's always too much going on at my parents' house.'

💜 Concise communication – when Sally felt in doubt, rather than accusing Steve of hiding his real thoughts on matters, she was simply to ask. She practised asking in a manner that was non-accusatory. For example, 'I'd like to know if you have any other reasons for making that choice?' Rather than, 'I don't believe that's your only reason for making that choice!'

♥ Identifying flashpoints – in exploring their styles of thinking it was clear that certain issues were more likely to cause problems for Sally and Steve. Interestingly these were the more personal ones like family, friends, and where their relationship was going. It was clear that work, sports, and hobbies were quite easily discussed. The personal issues were more difficult for Sally. She had a rather chequered relationship history having been a bit of a 'terrorist' in style. Personal issues got to her. So she and Steve made a pact to be more explicit over their thoughts when a personal flashpoint came up.

At the root of understanding the different types of thinking men and women typically use is clarity. If you can be clear with each other, this will lead to deeper understanding, enhanced communication, and a happier romance. Let's look at thinking behind deeper relationship issues after a couple have been together for a while.

## Typical Examples Of How Men And Women Think *Later* In Relationships

| Topic | Men's thoughts | Women's thoughts |
| --- | --- | --- |
| Living together | 'It could work as long as I can still golf on Saturdays! | 'What does it mean if we move in? Is marriage on the cards? |

| | | |
|---|---|---|
| | Permanent? We'll see.' | Will I get stuck with the household stuff? Best discuss!' |
| Attraction | 'She doesn't look like Julia Roberts when she wakes up!' | 'He really *is* good looking when he smiles. My friends agree, too. But he could make more effort with clothes.' |
| Self-image | 'I'm quite a good catch.' | 'I wonder if he took so long deciding about his "ex"? I still feel he has doubts about me. I've got to protect myself a bit more and think more confidently.' |
| Does he/she love me? | 'She does or she wouldn't be with me.' | 'I know he loves me but finds it hard to say so very often. When we argue, I worry about him getting doubts.' |

| What to do? | 'Anything to burn off some energy. I've been cooped up in the office.' | 'I'd really like to go with Jane and Sam. I worry he gets fed up with just my company most weekends.' |
| --- | --- | --- |
| Deeper issues | 'I could talk to her about my work problem.' | 'I want to ask him if he's ever been as close to another woman. I think we're getting close in some ways. Will I annoy him if I bring it up?' |

**Total number of thoughts = 8 versus 16**

**Type of thoughts = Still 'cut to the chase' (men) versus 'pre-planning for eventualities' (women)**

As you can see from the chart, even later on down the line, most men will still 'cut to the chase' when it comes to thinking about relationships. Of course we can never actually know what someone is thinking. Even when you two decide to co-operate and discuss the way you think, there's still room for romantic deception! If you're in love with a man who has a straightjacket around his mind, he may pay lip service to communication. He may say, 'Yes, funny you should bring that up, I was also thinking our relationship was getting more serious!'

When actually he was drifting along quite happily, enjoying your company but without thoughts of the future. Only *you* spurred him into action and he decided it was best not to confess to his real thoughts. The thoughts actually crossing his mind were: 'Uh-oh, I thought this was just an enjoyable situation. I guess I've got to face facts – she wants more!'

# Key Messages To Remember When Deciphering Men's Thinking

You can only improve things with the man in your life, if you remember the following:

- We do think differently! And in recognizing this our types of thinking can complement each other. We can learn from each other!

- One type of thinking is *not* better than another! You're both right – it's simply you and your make-up that guides your thought processes.

- When thinking becomes negative – a style of thinking only becomes a negative when a person will not open up their mind to the way the other thinks. And that could be either of you who refuses to acknowledge and understand the other's type of thinking.

Two heads are better than one! This saying did not evolve without good reason. Putting your two minds together can enrich your relationship by learning to see other possibilities. Think of the way people often solve problems at work – they put their minds together to come up with the best solution. The way you two think forms an important piece of your relationship puzzle. The first piece towards understanding men. Be aware of this!

First impressions – he will undoubtedly present himself in the best possible light when you first meet. We *all* do, don't we? It's part of the 'dance of romance'. Behind these first impressions his thinking will remain fairly constant cutting to the chase. 'I think she likes me so I'll take this further.'

# Tips To Get Into His Mind

Think twice before you ask him, 'What are you thinking about?' This really annoys men and you're unlikely to get a straight answer. Surprise him instead with your thoughts, 'I was just thinking...'

Think again before you try to read his mind. You can't! But you can start straightforward conversations and encourage him to talk.

💗 Get your thinking cap on – men's thoughts often go simply from A to B. If yours go from A to Z, think through how best to express this without complicating issues, problems, and dilemmas.

💗 Silence is golden! Men seem to bear silence better than we do. Don't always read this as a negative! If he needs a moment to collect his thoughts so that he can express them the way he'd like – allow it.

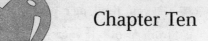

## Chapter Ten

# Understanding The Way Men Feel

So you're probably thinking right now that because you have some understanding of the way men think, you've won the battle. You've cracked men – thinking is the key to their behaviour. But it's not that simple. The way men feel about women, about you, and the way they feel when they're *in* relationships complicates understanding them. So open up to an interesting world – the world of men's feelings and enjoy the ride!

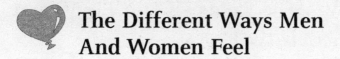

# The Different Ways Men And Women Feel

It's very common to hear a woman complain about a man that, 'He simply doesn't express his feelings!' Or, 'He doesn't seem to feel the way I do about things!' And even, 'Sometimes I don't think he has any feelings!' My answers to these are: 'true', 'true', and 'false' in that order.

First, he probably doesn't express his feelings. And if he does, he finds it difficult and gets a bit tongue-tied when trying. Or he does express his feelings but the woman has failed to see the signs of it. Second, he doesn't feel the way you do – and even another woman might not feel the same way. Feelings are very individual things! A common example is one woman might get extremely angry if her partner cheats, another gets incredibly depressed about cheating, and a third feels guilty herself, or any combination of these! Last, he does *have* feelings but he may quite simply keep them to himself – or as above, you may not be reading the signs correctly.

# The Roots Of Our Emotional Differences

The first step to understanding men's feelings is to go back to re-visit our ancient ancestors again. Recall how I described the inherent differences between men and women that meant we took on different roles. We got the initial child-rearing/cave-keeping role and they got to gallivant around the plains looking for meat or edible vegetation. This affected the way our different types of thinking developed but it also affected our ability to express feelings.

In our nurturing role, we needed to protect and care for our infants. This meant responding to their every need. These needs included feeding, cleaning, and generally needing comfort and so we had to 'be there' for the tiny dependants we were responsible for. And how were we able to respond? By being in tune with them at both practical and emotional levels. Being able to identify their emotions – from crying out to contentment – facilitated our own emotional development.

Now think of the men out hunting, fishing, farming, and collecting necessities for survival. Their over-riding responsibility was to get what was needed. As young boys, they were pushed out in an imperative way to assist the elders. The beginnings of emotional development and attachments were quickly relegated to second place in their daily quest to keep up with and learn from the men. Their purpose would not be served with too much questioning and evaluation, at an emotional level, of their daily tasks and lives. They had to get used to, for example, slaughtering a deer and not getting upset over how gory a task it was! Once again I don't wish to simplify the cultures and lifestyles of ancient peoples, but for our purposes keeping things direct is all we need to provide food for thought about the foundations of our modern lives and ways of interacting.

 # Modern Men And Feelings

So ancient men learned to 'get on with the job' and not express too much sentiment and this is how man has evolved for time ever after. After generations of rationalizing and even repressing emotions men frequently have difficulties with their feelings towards women. Just imagine if you'd repeatedly been given the message, both verbally and implied: 'You won't make the grade if you show weakness.' 'Weakness' of course meaning emotion! You can see it right from the arrival of a baby boy. When he takes his first tentative steps, trips, and scrapes his knee the mother's automatic reaction is: 'Big boys don't cry!' The mother then distracts them with some great big truck toy and says: 'Go on and finish digging that big hole in the sand you've started!'

Although we supposedly live in an age of emotional enlightenment where men are allowed to have feelings and express them, still there are far too many negative consequences for those who show, talk, and wear their feelings publicly. Too many men feel this negative pressure and notice the mixed messages women give out: 'I like a man who can discuss his feelings *but* I don't want a wimp!' 'How do we find that balance?' men wonder anxiously. And we are still only a generation away from men (the fathers of today's men) who did not talk about their feelings the way we'd hope all people could today. So our men today have been raised by those men of yesterday. All this talk of 'new men' actually is misleading because sadly there are still far fewer men around who are in touch with their feelings than those who have some difficulty with their feelings.

## The Potential Difficulties This Leads To

- Men may recognize they have feelings for you but don't want to delve too deeply into these. Life is so much easier for them when they don't feel pressurized to analyse these somewhat mysterious things.

- They may feel something but are not sure what or how serious it is – and leave off analysing them until they're pushed to. For example, a man may feel discomfort if he feels another man is paying too much attention to you. But he finds it hard to label – is this jealousy? Anger? Fear, perhaps?

- They may recognize strong feelings but are frightened by them. Then they start setting up defences before they've had the chance to define and label these feelings the way we would.

- In extreme cases, they may be so detached from their deeper feelings that they don't even enter into their relationship vocabulary – which has become very limited as a consequence.

## Typical Examples Of How Men And Women Feel *Early* In Relationships

Let's take a look at commonly reported feelings early in a relationship to see what you're up against.

| Topic | Men's feelings | Women's feelings |
| --- | --- | --- |
| First dates | 'I feel a bit wary.' | 'I feel so excited that I feel sick to my stomach! I feel so nervous!' |
| Attraction | 'I feel really attracted to her.' | 'I'm not sure how attracted I feel to him. I feel a bit funny in his company.' |

| | | |
|---|---|---|
| Self-image | 'I feel fine.' (Even if untrue!) | 'I feel so confused about my feelings! Sometimes I feel great. But then I feel useless when I get tongue-tied.' |
| Does he/she like me? | 'I feel sure she likes me.' | 'I feel so unsure – does he like me or want to go to bed with me? I'd die if that was the case.' |
| What to wear? | 'I feel quite handsome in this.' | 'I feel sexy in this but what if he doesn't like it?' |
| What to talk about? | 'I feel happy talking about work.' | 'I feel so nervous – what if I say something stupid? I want him to feel interested in what I have to say!' |

**Total number of feelings = 6 (men) versus 12 (women)**

**Type of feelings = 'Avoiding depth' versus 'encompassing possibilities'**

As the chart shows at this early stage of the game, men are unlikely to delve too deeply into their feelings. When feelings come to the surface, they're likely to push them back down into the deeper reaches of their subconscious mind. When explored, a typical response will be: 'There's no point in getting excited about a situation before you have more of the facts!' They're aware of feelings lurking within them but they keep them under control. This ties in with the behaviour of early man – there was no point getting excited about a deer until it was caught! The modern message men work with is 'get the relationship facts first and then go deeper'. Quite the opposite to how most women feel, if we're honest, huh? Most of us say: 'I *feel* something so there must be a relationship brewing!'

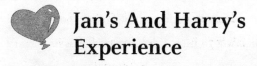 ## Jan's And Harry's Experience

Jan and Harry had quite a tumultuous affair going. They had never moved in together but spent most passion-filled nights together. Now by passion-filled I don't mean they were having an earth-shattering time in the bedroom – they were on a roller-coaster ride between a calm, affectionate relationship and grand arguments over his lack of 'emotional commitment'! Jan went around feeling hurt most of the time because Harry wasn't big on sharing his feelings. She wanted it all – from tender demonstrations of affection to big demonstrations of love – and every emotion in between described by him.

Harry couldn't understand what he termed her 'need for drama'. Typical of how many men feel: he was there wasn't he? He contributed to the relationship so what was the need for all this emotional stuff? He'd get angry because he felt Jan stirred things up on purpose to get some emotional combustion. Harry said he simply wanted a peaceful life. Jan said she did too. But peaceful to her meant being aware of how he was feeling about things – that would bring her peace of mind to relax! This expectation was stopping her reaching her relationship potential.

Things were coming to breaking point. Jan's rather 'too much, too soon' style had not been satisfied from the start. She'd recognized she'd dived in to the romantic waters and hoped at some point Harry would follow. Harry thought he'd followed! Only following to him didn't mean discussing every last feeling.

 ## Jan's And Harry's Relationship Enhancement Strategies

Jan and Harry had the basis for a good strong relationship. Quite simply the different ways they expressed their feelings got in the way. A bridge needed constructing between their two opposing emotional styles. Jan's being over-emotional and Harry's being quite frankly, typically male!

💜 Defining emotions – Jan felt she was good at defining her emotions. However, this didn't mean that this was necessarily the way for Harry to define his. Both were asked to keep a diary of emotions relating to the relationship for one week. For each entry, they noted the situation, how they felt, what the primary emotion was, and whether they verbalized it. Looking over these, it became clear that Jan defined her emotions with ease but Harry only did this at times when the emotion involved spontaneous affection. So if they shared a hug, he felt really happy. Or if Jan complimented him he felt content. If there was stress involved – like a disagreement over spending too much time with friends – Harry had far more difficulty both in identifying the primary emotion and certainly in verbalizing it. It felt like a mass of frustration rather than simply anger, or envy, or clearly both. This signposted the way for Harry to learn not to feel he had to conceal difficult emotions. In fact if earlier on, he'd expressed his frustration with Jan's 'too much, too soon' style, the issue may have been reconciled earlier.

💜 Negotiation of emotions – now it was time to encourage openness about what they felt. When Jan felt herself going into 'emotional-demanding' mode, she was to tell Harry she felt in need of some emotional dialogue. For example, this could possibly take the form of a little expression of his feelings of love for her. Harry was to do the same. If he was feeling emotional, he was to try to label this clearly for Jan. Step by step, emotional openness could be reached.

❤ Emotional acceptance – learning to live with each other's differences was an important task. Jan had to fight her feelings that Harry was somehow trying to upset her when he found it hard to express certain things or just didn't see it as necessary. And she came to acknowledge how valuable his brand of measured support had been on a number of occasions when she had work-related crises. Harry had to admit that some of Jan's emotionality could be great fun at parties when she could animate the conversation. Valuing their differences led them to see how complementary their pieces of the relationship puzzle were.

Emotional negotiation doesn't always go so smoothly. Let's suppose you are a relationship terrorist. You use emotions like a soldier uses hand-grenades. They are tossed around in an unpredictable fashion to upset the man you're seeing. A terrorist has a very subtle knowledge of how best to throw off the enemy and that's through the use of emotions. Things their present enemies (men) are already wary of! Terrorists simply reconfirm men's worst nightmare that some women are impossible to understand – and it rubs off on the rest of us! This is what happened in the next case study.

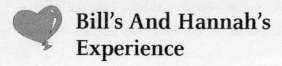

# Bill's And Hannah's Experience

When Bill met Hannah, she had a very suspect relationship track record. Hannah had left behind her a trail strewn with the remains of broken hearts. But was she happy with all the damage she'd inflicted? No! And with Bill, she had high hopes for her first relationship success.

Bill was really puzzled when they first began to disclose more intimate information, and learned more about the bits and pieces of her past. Here she was an intelligent, attractive woman: 'How could she have three broken engagements behind her?' he wondered. 'And why isn't she on speaking terms with any of her many ex-boyfriends?' Bill, himself, was a thoroughly decent man. He had the usual problems with talking about intimate things but at least he tried. But in some way the mystery of Hannah's conflicting nature actually served to spark Bill's interest. Frequently men who want to learn to express and share their emotions are drawn to women who seem to do this well. These men want a piece of the relationship puzzle that complements their emotional reserve. So in a sense opposites do attract in the right circumstances.

Unbeknownst to Bill, Hannah was fighting her own desperate battle inside herself *not* to jeopardize this relationship. The more understanding Bill tried to be, the more he tried to be a 'new man', the harder her battle got. Although Hannah used emotional confrontation and emotionally demanding behaviour to 'fight off' men, actually she was afraid of deeper emotions that might lead to intimacy. In her past, she had experienced real unhappiness within her family. Now what seemed to be a desire on her part to be emotional with men was actually her terrorist façade. Those that responded with tentative attempts to emotionally connect to Hannah were the ones who got dumped. Like the three different men she'd gone so far as to become engaged to!

It was now or never. Bill was ready to break off the relationship. He was confused by her emotional outbursts over seemingly straightforward issues. He also felt his attempts at emotional communication were being rebuffed – intelligent guy! After her bad behaviour, Hannah would plead for another chance. Typical terrorist behaviour – seeing how far she could go before he'd really never come back. But this time she really did want it to work. She wanted to accept his attempts at connecting with her. She wanted the emotions she showed to be a genuine reflection of her feelings.

So here we had a problem with Hannah's difficult emotions and Bill's exasperation at not being able to fathom her out. His emotions were straightforward as far as he was concerned. Well protected and kept in check, but straightforward! So between his male emotional straightjacket and her volatility there was much understanding to be sought.

## Bill's And Hannah's Relationship Enhancement Strategies

- Emotional honesty – Bill and Hannah made a pact of emotional honesty. No matter how scary it felt, both had to be honest about their real emotions. So if Hannah was trying to provoke an argument, she actually had to explain what was going on behind her argumentative behaviour – usually a feeling of confusion and fear. If Bill was feeling uneasy about expressing himself, he had to take the plunge and go ahead and do it. Each day they were to check with the other that they were prepared for a day of emotional honesty.

- Emotional balance – both needed to find better balance within themselves. Within herself, Hannah needed to achieve balance so that she didn't veer from one extreme behaviour to another. Bill needed to achieve balance between expressing his emotions and holding them back. Each was to recognize at an individual level when they thought they were achieving balance. This was to be noted down in their diaries. When they felt things weren't going well for them emotionally – they were getting out of balance – they were to look back at the diary entries. A moment's contemplation would take them back to the way they felt when they had balance.

♥ Emotional trading – Hannah and Bill agreed to try an emotional empathy exercise – 'trading places'. For a week, they were to practise trading, emotionally, each time an emotive issue arose. An emotive issue was defined very loosely. It could be annoyance at the toothpaste tube being squeezed in the middle right through to hurt feelings over a cutting remark. This emotional communication exercise was to help them learn to see how the other felt about things. At first, it was difficult particularly when Hannah was indifferent (a terrorist tactic that throws men off after some emotionally charged behaviour) one day to Bill's attempts at affection. He felt angry and she acted like she didn't care. Hannah was coaxed into the emotional trading by his goodwill though. On another occasion, Hannah coaxed Bill in a similar way to express some uncomfortable feelings she could guess he had. Emotional trading was a real learning experience because the person you are trying to empathize with needs to describe clearly what they're feeling. So better emotional communication is achieved.

## Typical Examples Of How Men and Women Feel *Later* In Relationships

So you've been going out with him for a number of months now but still wonder what he really feels. Consider these:

| Topic | Men's feelings | Women's feelings |
|-------|----------------|------------------|
| Living together | 'I feel a bit wary. What does this really mean?' | 'I feel so excited. I wonder if he knows how much this means to our future. It feels like a turning point to me.' |
| Attraction | 'I feel attracted to her particularly in our quiet moments.' | 'The more I know him, the more I feel attracted to him. It's amazing how that works. His smile and laugh are infectious!' |
| Self-image | 'I feel good about myself. She makes me feel good.' | 'I feel really confident in some ways. But then again I feel really scared at times – does he want this to last?' |
| Does he/she love me? | 'She does – I can tell. Why else would we have lasted?' | 'Most of the time I can feel his love. Other times I feel he's not that deeply involved. I wish I knew his real feelings.' |

| Deeper Issues | 'I feel happy talking to her about most things. Just don't get her on the topic of our relationship!' | 'I feel he'd run a mile if I told him my most intimate thoughts. I feel this blocks us getting really intimate.' |

**Total number of feelings = 9 (men) versus 12 (women)**
**Type of feelings = 'Masculine depth' versus 'encompassing possibilities'**

As you can see the rate of feelings expressed by men has increased from the early stages. There is less questioning though and also less emphasis on where the relationship is going than the typical feelings expressed by women. Look at the example, 'Does she love me?' and a typical response is, 'We're together aren't we? So she must.' His clarity comes from the fact the relationship just 'is' – it exists. It doesn't necessarily explore the varying nature of feelings, as does the typical response of a woman.

In looking at this piece of the relationship puzzle – that is the way men feel things differently – you need to remember that years and years of conditioning to ignore/suppress their emotions is not going to change overnight, regardless of how important *you* are to a man. Emotional habits don't change that easily.

Think about an emotional habit you may have. Maybe you fly off the handle and erupt with anger under stress. Or maybe you get sick with nerves caused by feelings of insecurity before every first date. Have you been able to change these emotional habits? If you're honest, you'll know how hard these are to break. The first step is recognizing the way you react emotionally. The next step is trying to substitute these feelings with more positive ones. And then it's a constant battle to keep this up until the new, more positive approach becomes the habit. Understanding how difficult it is to change the way you feel, and express these feelings, will go a long way to helping you understand the men you meet. This will help you reach your relationship potential!

 ## Key Messages To Remember When Trying To Understand Men's Emotions

We experience emotions differently! We believe they're something to be expressed and so we explore them. Most men believe they're something to be repressed and so ignore them! It's explore versus ignore.

A lifetime of programming – there's always hope that the man you fall in love with may express his feelings or learn to. But you will *not* change a lifetime of emotional programming overnight.

Emotions at face value – what you see is what you get. Just because you have a dozen different emotions racing through your heart does not mean he will. Years of repression leads to fewer emotions being experienced. Most men simply operate within relationships at a less emotional level. Emotions are there, of course, usually somewhere deep down but they don't dwell on them – 'The relationship is working so let's not get over excited.' 'There are problems but let's not get bogged down with them.'

Lack of emotional display doesn't equal lack of commitment! Just because most men do *not* display their emotions to the extent we do doesn't mean they aren't committed. Quite the contrary. Men in some ways end up more committed than women. Once they've taken the plunge, which is very scary for lots of men, they don't want to let go lightly. Men report falling in love fewer times in a lifetime than women. But once they fall, the comfort they derive from a relationship is very real. You simply need to look at divorce statistics to see that more women seek divorce than men.

What happens when he won't open up? You may be with a man who in the end won't commit to actively working with you on this part of your relationship – unlike Harry and Bill. If his other qualities outweigh his uneasiness to learn to express deeper emotions, then you will have to go with the flow. Without pressure, over time, he may grow to feel more comfortable with his emotions. However, if he's there for you, if he's good company, and you love him, you'll simply have to keep playing the guessing game: 'What is he feeling right now?' Or get on with enjoying him for who he is.

 # Tips To Get Into His Feelings

💜 Ask what he thinks and you might be able to work out what he feels!

💜 Feel free to tell him your feelings but in moderate doses! Many women complain their partners spend more time with their male friends. It's not surprising when you won't allow him the space to simply be with you.

💜 Feel lucky if he talks about his feelings. With a measured, rather than a 'Oh-my-gosh,-he's-opened-up-to-me.-Now-I-can-bombard-him-with-questions!' excited response, he will open up even more.

💜 Compare his feelings to someone he admires. You may say something like: 'I bet Gascoigne felt like that when he gave that goal away,' and it may make him feel able to express himself like his role model. Although if his role model isn't Gazza, you don't stand much chance!

Chapter Eleven

# Understanding Men And Sex

Yes, we're finally here – sex! That element of our human nature that probably drives the biggest wedge into the already large male-female divide. Why when sex is supposed to be such a pleasurable pursuit, between two loving individuals, do we hear constant talk of sexual problems? If it's not your best friend complaining that her partner, 'Rolls over straight afterwards without a thought to what I might be feeling,' then it's your sister complaining that, 'He's as sensitive as a jackhammer drilling up the pavement!'

From the man's point of view, a woman's bedroom behaviour is just as problematic. Complaints range from, 'I just can't seem to satisfy her in the bedroom,' to, 'I'm not sure what she really wants. Sometimes I think she wants it as if we're strangers who've fallen into bed for some earthy sex. Other times I'm supposed to be some sort of Don Juan – all roses and romance!'

As you listen to what one sex has to say about the other, it becomes clear that our sexual attitudes differ in many ways. But rather than relish their differences, men and women seem confused and overwhelmed by them. Many relationships have sunk in the romantic waters due to sexual problems. The bedroom often comes to mirror what the rest of the relationship is like. And why is this? Because sexual problems can seem so immediate, so intensely intimate, and so central to the way two people feel about each other, and themselves, that this is where the struggle to assert yourself within the relationship often begins. Although sexual differences are less frequently cited in divorce cases, certainly in the counselling arena sexual difficulties come to the fore.

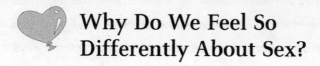

# Why Do We Feel So Differently About Sex?

Yes, we are going to go back to our favourite people – our ancient ancestors to shed some light on this complicated subject. Think about our female predecessors – what did sexual relations mean to them? Well it wasn't all about orgasms (although they might have helped spark their interest in getting close to a man. And certainly helped along the process of fertilization!). It was more about babies. Successful sexual relations resulted in pregnancy and the propagation of the species. And what did pregnancy, birth, and child-rearing mean to ancient women? Sexual relations, leading to these events, meant a complete change of life for women. They resulted in a woman's nurturing side being developed as we've discussed in the last two chapters.

And what about ancient men? Sexual relations meant their innate desire to father offspring was met. And as ancient men were often on the move in their search for food and greener pastures, it meant a lot of time being spent away from the mother of their children. It's believed they probably 'sowed their seed' many times over with different partners. As women were quite literally left 'holding the baby', it was more of an imperative for them to try to maintain a relationship with the father of their children. That relationship ensured a food source, and that protection from the elements was provided while they were still tied to young children. And that gave us our early training in associating all our interactions, even sexual ones, with forming relationships.

Thus the seeds were sown for differences between the sexes to grow in terms of what sexual relations meant to them. In our modern lives you can still recognize the echo from the past – the behaviours of the ancients rooted deeply in our psyches. On the whole women do not detach emotional involvement from sexual relations. Because sexual relations, even with modern birth control, still have the connotation of creating a life-long role of motherhood as a possible result. Of course it is more complicated than that. In the way women think and feel, we are still generally more geared to provide a nurturing environment for a relationship to develop. Even when interest is initially sparked by sexual attraction across a crowded nightclub! And although modern women are free to engage in whatever sexual activity they want to, many cannot deny the existence of special feelings for a lover – even if only a transitory one.

Men on the other hand with their ability to 'cut to the chase', in their thinking and feeling, can and will frequently detach their emotions from sexual encounters. This is not to denigrate in any way the many men who place a high emotional value on sexual relations. However, the majority, particularly when younger, are able to experiment and dabble in sexual relationships without considering emotional attachment in much depth. Which would be the icing on the relationship cake for many women!

## 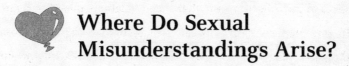 Where Do Sexual Misunderstandings Arise?

If we know that men and women have basic differences in their feelings about sex, why are there still so many misunderstandings? Because most people are still liable to approach the sexual aspect of their relationships from their point of view! To see them the way they want to without considering how the other does. I hope by this point *you* are starting to see how the differences between the way men and women think, feel, and approach sexual relations are important to consider if you want a relationship to succeed. You can't have it all your way – your two puzzle pieces have to fit snuggly together with their different yet complementary shapes!

Sexual misunderstandings stem from two main areas. Firstly they stem from differences in overall expectations about sex. Expectations of what it should be like ('amazing' women think – 'satisfying' men think), when it should happen ('at the right moment' women think – 'any time' men think), and what should be the result ('a deeper relationship' women think – 'a no-strings romp' men think!) etc., differ between the sexes. Secondly a lack of sexual communication is at the root of misunderstandings. Because so many people find it hard to talk about sexual matters many wires get crossed in the process. Sexual expectations and communication are linked in many ways.

##  Sexual Expectations – Women's

Thinking about the first issue – sexual expectations – we women have to put our hands up and admit to shaping our bedroom behaviour to suit our mood and then expecting our partners to understand this. For example, if you're riding high on some accomplishment at work, you may rush home wanting fast and furious sex. This reconfirms your sense of making things happen. If you're feeling sensitive, you may quietly slip between the sheets and expect to be treated like a delicate flower. And the men are supposed to conform to these expectations.

And another expectation of ours is that men will feel the same way we do when actually making love! Well that myth should have been exploded in the last chapter on men's emotions. Remember the message – they don't necessarily feel things the way we do! So let's stay with that message. Even if you and your partner are in a committed, stable, loving relationship, when you make love you two will *not* feel the same way. Just because you might be feeling romantic and expect it to be all 'hearts and flowers' inside, he may simply be enjoying the physical sensations of making love to you! Of course he may also be getting more emotional about it, too, but even so he's less likely to go on and express this.

 # Sexual Expectations – Men's

And what are men's expectations like? Extremely varied is the answer. However, research that examines men's expectations of sexual relations finds most admit that very often they simply expect a 'bit of fun', and 'some sexual release', or have sex because their friends *expect* them to! Yes, men are more likely to have their *own* sexual expectations shaped by those of their peer group. Sounds pretty weak, huh? And it is. But that's how men can be! There is still more pressure on men to be seen to be having sex whether in or out of a relationship.

Another thing to bear in mind is that men often expect sex to be relatively easy – it should *only* involve pleasure. Working for it, or for mutual pleasure, is low on most men's list. They don't necessarily want to complicate it with lots of trimmings. I'm not just talking foreplay here, although that is a good example of this. But everything else that we might expect to go with sex, they don't necessarily expect too. So, for example, the fact we may want to talk a bit before lovemaking, or after for that matter, is not necessarily on their list of expectations.

Talking about foreplay, where do you think all this business comes from? Why did this become such a hot issue after the sexual revolution of the 1960s? Because of course it was suddenly all right for a woman to acknowledge her sexual feelings and with this her expectations of what sex should be like. Foreplay became an issue between men and women representing these different expectations. Women expected what men often thought was extravagant – foreplay!

 ## Sexual Communication

The second main area of misunderstanding involves sexual communication. Although nowadays we all have more sexual freedom, this doesn't mean a good vocabulary has grown up around this increased choice. As men and women think and feel differently, this affects what they communicate! There's lots of scope for difficulties. How do they communicate differently? I think it would be easiest to refer you to the tables for some common examples.

# Male Sexual Communication

Let's look at the sorts of things men say and do *early* on in a relationship and what they mean in terms of their sexual attitudes:

| What they say | What they mean |
| --- | --- |
| 'You look great tonight!' | 'Wonder what she's like in bed?' |
| 'I really care about you.' | 'I care about this evening going well.' |
| 'I'm looking for commitment.' | 'I might want commitment.' |
| 'I believe women should express themselves.' | 'Please don't say, "No"!' |
| 'Do you like me?' | 'Do you want to go to bed with me?' |
| 'My last girlfriend was demanding in bed.' | 'She wanted lots of foreplay.' |
| 'I think people "know" early on.' | 'Sex will help us tell if we like each other.' |
| 'I don't want to pressure you!' | 'I don't want to wait forever!' |

And there's non-verbal sexual communication too:

| What they do | What they mean |
| --- | --- |
| Put their arm around you. | 'You're mine – let's go to bed.' |
| Nuzzle your ear. | 'Let's get intimate.' |
| Tickle you. | 'I'll get your defences down.' |
| Kiss you gently. | 'Let's get going.' |
| Kiss you passionately. | 'Let's do it now.' |

I'm sure you get my drift by now! All the above, from the two tables, you may misread to mean that they've got to have *you*! But they're actually communicating: 'I've got to have sex!' Men would like to keep a sexual relationship as simple as possible. If it goes along nicely, then they're liable to fall for you. Or if you're into the waiting game and won't go to bed with a man until you're satisfied with the emotional connection you're making, they'll wait – as long as they like you enough. Otherwise they'll be looking for a quick exit. And that may not mean they don't like you enough to wait. It may mean they're simply not into anything more than casual sex at this point.

In many ways men look at the sexual part of a relationship in the opposite way to women. Women often feel that if the emotional connection is good then the sex will be, too. Men think that if the sex is good then the emotion might follow. Unless they're made to wait, as above, and then they'll weigh up whether the wait is worth it.

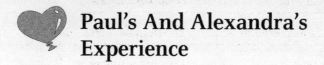

# Paul's And Alexandra's Experience

Alexandra and Paul illustrate the paradox above – coming to the sexual part of their relationship from opposite corners. Alexandra had always believed that sex was secondary in a relationship. For her, an emotional commitment was necessary before she went to bed with someone. Sex could only be good if the emotions were in place first. Many of her friends had discarded this sort of view and romped through many flings. To Alexandra, they didn't necessarily seem any happier for it. Paul believed that good sex was great and could bring two people emotionally closer.

When Alexandra met Paul, she'd just come out of an unhappy relationship. After misreading her ex-boyfriend's signs to mean he was getting emotionally close to her, Alexandra started sleeping with him. Time went on and nothing seemed to get deeper. Then she found out her 'ex' was happy dating, happy having sex, but had no intention of committing to a full-on relationship – reinforcing her already 'too little, too late' style.

This had left her very wary of men's motives and it confirmed to her that emotional connection was more important than ever. She wanted to find a man on the same wavelength.

Paul was going to pay a price. Alexandra seemed to analyse all he said and did. But because she was analysing him from her own perspective – putting her own way of thinking about sex and feelings on to him – she didn't get very far. Instead they were both getting annoyed and confused about the situation.

Alexandra was annoyed because she really liked him and wanted the relationship to move forward. But every time he made a move to deepen the physical part of the relationship, she challenged him. She began to doubt the way she approached relationships. Paul was annoyed because he felt he was being punished for her ex-boyfriend. How could they build up a full relationship when she didn't have any trust?

## Alexandra's And Paul's Relationship Enhancement Strategies

Alexandra and Paul needed to bridge the sexual divide of *when* a sexual relationship should begin. When faced with this divide, there are a number of things to consider:

❤ Sexual confidence – always be confident of your sexual relationship beliefs. They're important and shouldn't be judged negatively. A different attitude about when to start a sexual relationship was not reason enough for Alexandra to doubt herself. Alexandra needed to re-affirm her right to her beliefs. Communicate your attitudes clearly to a man. If you don't want sex before you're sure of an emotional commitment, spell this out at an appropriate time. You two may be snuggled up on a Sunday afternoon, as he nuzzles you (remember this means, 'Let's get intimate' from the previous table!), you can calmly say something like, 'I love snuggling up but I don't want to rush into anything sexual.'

❤ Sexual pressure – be prepared for pressure – some is to be expected. Although there are a few unique men out there who won't pressure you at all! Keep your boundaries where *you* want them. Too much pressure that makes you feel uncomfortable is a clear sign he wants sex, and at any cost – your well-being! He's either too selfish or too immature to be involved with. You may try and ride this type of pressure out but be warned – you're unlikely to come out with the sort of relationship you want. Alexandra felt some pressure from Paul but in the end believed it was an acceptable level – he was simply expressing his desire for her without overwhelming her. Once they'd talked about the issue of pressure, both were more aware of the other's feelings.

❤ Recognize differences – particularly in the way you two see sex fitting into a new relationship. But if you can acknowledge these differences it can work. The openness Paul and Alexandra were developing reassured each other of their feelings and motives. If a man doesn't feel everything that you feel – waves splashing, moonbeams dancing, etc. – it doesn't mean that sex between you two isn't a good thing. He may enjoy it in his way!

♥ Respect each other – your new partner should not be punished for how an 'ex' treated you. Alexandra owned up to treating Paul with little respect – assuming he was going to be like her 'ex'. In the end this opened up enough honesty for them to bridge the divide in their sexual beliefs.

♥ Deal with the heartache of the past – don't come loaded with emotional baggage to a new relationship. It was a bit late in Alexandra's case as she now acknowledged she probably should have had more time before getting involved again. You need time out from relationships, if past hurt is clouding how you see and communicate with a new man. If there's one thing a male ego hates – that's to be compared to an 'ex'. Or you assuming he's going to be just like an 'ex'. And this goes for sexual performance, too! You definitely have terrorist tendencies, if you tell your new lover how great your old one was.

♥ Don't use sex for ulterior motives – if you're up for sex early in a relationship that's your right! But don't use sex to try to capture him – it may do the opposite. Many men still hold a double standard: 'If she has sex with me early on, then she probably would with anyone!' So in their own odd, male way, they will try it on but actually want something of a chase! And don't use sex to get affection. Use affection to get affection – there's nothing wrong with lots of kisses and cuddles as long as you're clear what your boundaries are. Alexandra and Paul learned how to discuss where affection left the equation and sex entered into it. That is, how they both felt about the link between affection and sex.

## Typical Examples Of Men's Sexual Attitudes *Later* In Relationships

So you've been going out with him for a number of months now but still wonder what he really feels in terms of sex. Let's look at what men say and what they mean *later* on in a relationship.

| What they say | What they mean |
| --- | --- |
| 'You look great tonight.' | 'I wonder if we'll have sex tonight?' |
| 'Of course I like/love you.' | 'At least enough to see how far this might go.' |
| 'We seem to be getting serious.' | 'You seem to want commitment.' |
| 'I'm interested in how you feel.' | 'Just tell me after we go to bed!' |
| 'Sometimes it would be nice to let go.' | 'Animal sex and quickies would do just fine!' |
| 'Compatibility is important.' | 'Compatibility in bed is important.' |
| 'We'll only go as far as you want.' | 'We'll go as far as I can get you to go.' |

| | |
|---|---|
| 'I'm up for trying something new.' | 'What's wrong with what we're doing.' |
| 'Am I giving you enough foreplay?' | 'You don't really want any more foreplay, do you?' |
| 'Do I satisfy you?' | 'Tell me I'm good!' |

As the chart shows at this later stage men are still unlikely to want things to get too complicated. 'Sex is for pleasure, right? Let's not complicate pleasure with the serious business of emotions!' they think. They will, though, make noises as if they're thinking in that direction. That is, most men know they should appear to be giving some thought to how the relationship is going and in terms of linking sex to the emotional side of things.

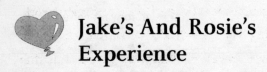

## Jake's And Rosie's Experience

Because men are less likely to discuss their feelings about your sexual relationship and how it links into your overall relationship, even at later stages this can cause problems. Jake and Rosie are an example of how a sexual relationship can become a problem later in a relationship when two people have different expectations.

Rosie and Jake had been together for six months when trouble started. Rosie felt she had a good understanding of men and sensed that Jake was deeply emotionally involved with her. She had enough romantic intelligence to know that sometimes you could sense these things even if they were unspoken. When encouraged he'd talk about their relationship and what the future may or may not hold. And this was enough as she knew he cared deeply for her. They'd started making love when they'd been together about three weeks and all seemed good. They enjoyed a true passion stage that lasted about three months where they couldn't seem to keep their hands off each other.

Now though Rosie felt differently. It seemed to her that Jake wanted sex all the time. 'How could it "mean" something to him when it could be just any old sex?' she wondered. As far as she was concerned the deeper they got into the relationship, the more meaningful sex became to her. And meaningful did not include quick sex in the morning before rushing to work. Or quick sex during advertisements on television between the main programme. What she didn't understand was that because the relationship was getting deeper, he felt a free connection with her and enjoyed spontaneous sex as well as the more romantic variety that involved lots of affection and foreplay. His attitude being: 'When we have something so good why not show it through sex?'

This tension was leading her back into her old controlling style. Something she'd fought against as she'd learned more about men and herself. In the past, she'd enjoyed quite a butterfly pattern that had actually led to a lot of heartache. Rosie couldn't control all these men at once!

## 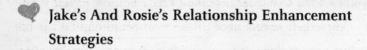 Jake's And Rosie's Relationship Enhancement Strategies

It's important to bridge the sexual divide of *when* you two have different sexual expectations:

- Sex and emotional depth – in Rosie's scheme of things, 'sex drive' shouldn't be mistaken for a measure of emotional depth. Yet this is precisely how Jake saw it! She simply couldn't see the way he approached sex. That for him the depth of the relationship was enhanced by sexual variety of all kinds. You can't force each other to see sex in the same way but you can *understand* each other's point of view. Both noted down a list of adjectives that described their experience of sex. Exploring these lists allowed them both to see and understand the differences between them.

- Sexual expectations – when sexual expectations seem to be a problem, you can gently and tactfully broach the subject. Rosie wanted to handle their differences in a way that wouldn't upset Jake. Remember men are extremely sensitive to any suggestions you don't want sex as frequently as they do. It's important to emphasize the positives you feel. This will then lead you gently into territory that otherwise may be taken negatively by him!

💝 Sexual feelings – each time you make love, you may feel it's special. You need to face facts that with men sex in itself can often be enough – nothing more, nothing less. If it satisfies their sexual need at the moment, then that's good enough for them. Jake learned to show more affection after lovemaking – even if it had been of the quicker variety. More affection allowed Rosie to feel emotionally appreciated no matter when or where the lovemaking took place.

💝 Continual appraisal – as time goes by in a relationship, it is often the woman who feels things are being taken for granted at a sexual level. Men are often happy to slip into a lovemaking routine that is pleasurable but not particularly creative. As long as sex is regular, it appears to meet their needs. Whereas we place so much stock on it being special that it seems we want it to constantly evolve. Expressing this expectation as the relationship develops will at least create an air of honesty. Too many women get frustrated by this, but they won't communicate these feelings and let their partner know! Rosie used a 'lead by example' technique. She accepted the role of leader in carefully guiding their lovemaking into new pastures over time.

💝 Acceptance – Rosie and Jake managed to learn to accept each other's needs were different in the long term. Jake needed to verbalize feelings of emotional attachment to her particularly at intimate moments. And Rosie needed to accept that sometimes a quickie would be what was on

Jake's menu – and no reflection on the depth of his feelings for her!

As you are now aware, men's sexual feelings present a mine-field of problems. Mainly because we, as women, feel lovemaking forms a special part of a relationship and would like that confirmed by them, too. We so want things to be equal in our relationships – and that means feeling equally overwhelmed by the emotions of lovemaking! But we're too fair-minded! Why can't we happily enjoy, and even selfishly hog, the depth and range of our emotions during intimacy? As our sexual relationship strikes to the very core of ourselves, acknowledging these differences will help you put in place another piece of the relationship puzzle. To help you with this, here are some things to remember.

## Some Key Messages To Remember About Men And Sex

What men want to hear – they love heaps of praise (so do we!) and any problem should be tackled first by telling him how great he is in bed. They can detach their emotions from sex – but not their egos!

- What men feel before sex – they are focused on their 'cut-to-the-chase' mode of thinking. 'Will sex happen?' they wonder. Their feelings will extend as far as, 'I feel really horny!'

- What men feel during sex – they are almost totally focused on the physical sensations they are feeling. These include how you feel to them, 'She's so soft,' to how they feel, 'This feels great!' They are unlikely to be feeling things like, 'I'm so in love and this lovemaking confirms that!'

- What men feel after sex – usually they feel contentment. Again they are focused on their physical feelings, 'I feel exhausted – time to have a snooze!' They are unlikely to lie there feeling a rosy glow of intimate emotions. You'll have to be satisfied with contentment!

- Sexual attraction – you may wonder what your 'ex' sees in his new girlfriend. Possibly she doesn't demand emotional affirmation every time they go to bed together!

- Don't insist on sharing your emotions of the moment – if they've got an arm around you, lying in a haze of contentment, they're likely to feel annoyed if you want to share your feelings of what it was like. 'It's done, it was good, what more does she want?' they think.

- If it's on offer – he'll take it! But if you want more than a fling better to get an idea of his intentions.

- His most basic sexual thought – 'If it feels good, then why not do it?'

- Men see sex as a performance art! Yes, it's true men link sex with performance. And that means their performance overall as a man. So any problems in the bedroom between the two of you and inside he's likely to feel pretty useless.

- Sex will deepen your relationship! He may really believe he can't know his feelings about you without trying out the bedroom first. You can of course choose to soften his approach by timing going to bed with him when, and only when, you feel comfortable. If at a deep level his feelings about where sex fits into a relationship really go against your beliefs, then this may become an insurmountable hurdle. Meaningful compromise is possible with most couples and will help you reach the heart of your relationship potential.

# Understanding Men And Romance

I hate to let you in on something, girls, but if you think 'men and sex' was a tricky subject, 'men and romance' is even more confusing! At least with sex, men feel they're aiming for a goal. There's a known quantity at the end of the tunnel – sexual satisfaction. And that is a rather big and understandable pay-off for men! But with romance – what do they get at the end of it? Is it something tangible? Not necessarily. Is it something they can measure? No, it isn't. And that's where the trouble lies. Men are such practical creatures at heart that something romantic is a bit of a mystery to them.

Men start to wonder, 'Why is romance so important to women? It lacks direction, there's no real goal, 'What's the big deal?' But that's just it – the attitude that summarizes our differences. We love romance just because it *is* an added extra bit of wonderful fun! There doesn't have to be a point except to make you feel loved, valued, adored, even gorgeously soppy inside! That's good enough reason for us women to want to create a romantic atmosphere because we know such delicious feelings sets our relationship apart from others. If we're made to feel special, it will propel an ordinary relationship into the realms of a wonderful relationship.

Men (or at least most men) just don't get it. And that's why romance becomes a bit of a game. Men aren't sure of what the game plan is – so they guess! Because what we mean by romance doesn't fit neatly into a tidy 'action-result' plan, they make it up as they go. That's why you hear women complain, 'His idea of romance is a box of chocolates on our anniversary!' or, 'He never simply surprises me – it's flowers on birthdays and anniversaries like clockwork!'

Sometimes the easiest, traditional solutions (flowers and chocolates) seem a quick fix to men. They think they're being romantic. And we then think they aren't really committed to the principle! It boils down to most men wanting the relation-ship to feel good, to feel comfortable. Of course many realize that if being romantic makes the woman feel good that posi-tive feeling spins off on them, so they try.

There is hope – once they get the hang of being romantic in ways that we encourage! And we need to be fair to them. Often men make gestures that we wouldn't consider romantic but they do. By doing things for us (fixing, tinkering, etc.), they feel they're demonstrating their love. We simply prefer demon-strations that are less practical and more special. Understanding such differences will help you reach your relationship potential.

 # Why Do We Get So Worked Up About Romance?

Why when romance is supposed to be fun, spontaneous, and pleasurable, do we get so worked up about it? And I do mean seriously worked up – I've known relationships that have failed over the romance hurdle – she didn't get 'any', and he got tired of the non-too subtle hints for romance. Women do take it very seriously because somehow we've managed to get our self-worth wrapped up with this one. 'If I was a wonderful, desir-able woman then he'd be sweeping me off my feet with romantic surprises,' we think.

It also becomes a bit of a competition between women when discussing their partners. A sort of 'keeping-up-with-the-Joneses' scenario but instead it's: 'Who's got the most romantic guy, and so who's the most desirable woman!?' Conversations go something like: 'Stephen surprised me with flowers in my favourite colour – and they were so hard to get because they were out of season!'

'But my James had the restaurant bake a birthday cake for my birthday with little teddy bears on it!'

'Well remember when Stephen surprised me when I was in bed with flu with a singing telegram who sang *our* song while tap-dancing – just to make me laugh?' And so it goes on! *We* like to think *our* guy thinks we're the most special honey-bunny in the world and then we like to flaunt it to friends.

It's a continuation of when you're younger comparing what your parents got you for Christmas with your friends. And there was always one very sad little girl who wandered off from the crowd because her parents had failed to get her the latest Barbie! Well, don't despair if your partner isn't the most roman-tic man because as you will see there's always room for encour-aging a little more romance.

So we've been guilty of buying into the myth that somehow his level of romantic gestures reflects our level of worthiness! Instead we should be looking at romance as the delicious extra it should be and not a reflection of his love for us – because it's not! We'd be in a sorry state if romance did reflect men's true depth of feeling.

 ## Why Do Men And Women Place Different Values On Romance?

So why do we feel more intensely about the romantic element of our relationships than men? Well it certainly wasn't originally in our genes! Ancient man didn't arrive back from a hunt, bearing a slain wild boar dressed up with a wreath of leaves and an apple in its mouth just to show his cavewoman how much he loved her! No, romance grew along with the finer aspects of 'civilization'. As we put on more clothes, we put on more manners. Courtship became a ritual – a dance. It became the dance of romance. No longer could men simply claim a woman and take her to bed, or families palm off their daughters without much ado!

As courtship became refined so did the art of romance. At many points in history romance and courtship rituals became very elaborate. Think of Marc Anthony sweeping Cleopatra off her feet. Think of the French court before the French Revolution or 'Dandy' England. All sorts of elaborate and grand gestures, subterfuge and game playing went on in the name of romance. The whole point was to intensify desire between two lovers or potential lovers. It also was a bit of a gossiping point and people made reputations for themselves on the basis of their seduction abilities. Their seduction abilities depended on their romantic creativity!

Romance, as it was then, *did* reflect on a woman's desirability. You would become a great talking point (something to be desired in many societies of days gone by), if people referred to men's antics to win your heart. In this way an unspoken competition developed between women to prove how desirable they were. Such intensity of feeling over generations and the myths of society are hard to shake off, even for modern women. And all of us modern women grew up on a diet of fairy tales about princes sweeping their princesses off their feet – those fairy tales have a lot to answer for!

As well as the fairy tales, we grew up seeing loads of black and white 'weepies' – movies where dashing leading men like Clark Gable and Cary Grant got their women through amazing gestures of love. It's no wonder our 'inner child' absorbed this romantic side more than the guys! Why, if this is *not* the case, do we still have 'chick flicks' or 'girlie movies' as people call them? Because we love having our romantic side appealed to by seeing Meg Ryan fall in love in *Sleepless in Seattle* and Julia Roberts getting the man she loves in *Pretty Woman.*

# Why Have We Lost The Art Of Romance?

At points in history, romance became a fine art sadly to be lost over the generations within our memory. In the decades since the war, changing attitudes in society mainly about women and our roles meant that we no longer wanted to be seen as 'treasures' to be 'won' in a romantic game. Rather we wanted to be seen as equals in relationships. And that's a good thing except it has left us in the present state of confusion over romance and the etiquette of what we should or shouldn't do.

But still there's that part of our nature that longs for the hint of possibility, the slow seduction to a point of no return, and delicious demonstrations of love. We want to feel special particularly with the grind of living together. Romance is what helps keep a relationship alive and stops you from becoming simply flatmates! As far as men are concerned now that romance isn't something to be cultivated, as it was in earlier eras, they face a major problem of the fact that to be romantic means to show their feelings. And we know what difficulty many men encounter with those!

Many men claim that romance isn't important and women don't *really* want it, in these times of equality, do they? So they try and squirm out of it, at least until they're sure of their feelings. Actually they're missing the point – we want some romance as well as the career, the earnings, and everything else we expect as individuals! Once again, they do things back to front compared to us. Romantic gestures that strike the right chord if anything are going to intensify our feelings – whereas they want to wait until they're sure of their feelings before they go out on a romantic limb. Romance to them simply makes them vulnerable. They have a great fear of being found out too early at an emotional level. Then they'll be at our mercy because we'll know they're involved with us.

This is why romance has become a guessing game. Men are cagey about the gestures they make and the meaning they may be giving away. And sometimes they're quite amazed by what women find to be romantic. Picture this: five years into your relationship you chat over the early days. You happen to mention how romantic it was the first time he called you 'my beautiful bandy legs' (the pet nickname he gave you the first time you made love!). He looks at you totally bewildered and asks, 'You thought that was romantic?'

Then you go on to tell him how the way he used to stroke your hair absent-mindedly while watching a film used to make you feel so warm inside. It felt as if he couldn't believe how soft it was and couldn't resist touching it. And he says something like he assumed flowers and chocolates were the gestures you liked! So another man is put on the correct path of romance. That many wonderful romantic moments have nothing to do with purchasing gifts like flowers!

 # What Happens When We First Meet A Potential Partner?

Most women come to learn that sometimes through a subtle and skilful use of largely non-verbal communication, we can coax men into demonstrating their feelings for us. These demonstrations take the form of gestures that begin to show their level of commitment. For example, these may be traditional gestures like giving flowers, or helpful gestures like fixing something for you. Men may see the latter as romantic so it's our duty to show them otherwise! What makes some of these gestures special is the romantic element they contain. It's very frustrating, though, because a lot of men fight against this subtle form of romantic coercion. And that's when women begin to feel hurt or as if he's not really interested in their feelings. Of course there are some true exceptions to the rule and some lucky women don't have to coax, coerce, or push their partner into getting romantic.

# Romantic Gestures – What Men Do And What It Means

Let's take a look at romantic gestures men are likely to make and what they symbolize:

| What men do | What they mean |
| --- | --- |
| Gives any old flowers. | 'I have to do this, don't I?' |
| Gives your favourite flowers. | 'I "might" care.' |
| Gives chocolates. | 'I'm a caring guy with no imagination.' |
| Gives you a cuddly toy. | 'I really am a soppy git dressed up as a "hard"man!' |
| Gives you a pet nickname. | 'I think you're nice/cute/sweet.' |
| Arranges a surprise meal. | 'I care.' |
| Arranges one with candles. | 'I care and I'm thoughtful.' |
| Arranges a surprise outing. | 'Help, I'm beginning to get vulnerable!' |
| Sends a love letter. | 'I'm vulnerable but getting comfortable with it!' |
| Shows public affection/caring. | 'I'm losing all sense of caution.' |
| Anything more unusual. | 'I've fallen hook, line, and sinker, and it's scary!' |

As the gestures get larger, or more 'out there', so his willingness to become vulnerable increases. This is the time when things need to be handled with care. He needs loads of reassurance and encouragement. Then he'll find out that it's not so bad after all making you feel good through romance.

 ## Joan's And Michael's Experience

Joan, 34, was a die-hard romantic with strict 'criteria' for the men she dated. If they didn't make romantic gestures soon enough, she would dump them. She had an intense 'too much, too soon' style. And if it wasn't satisfied by reciprocal intensity in the form of lots of romance, her patience wore thin. Looking at her pattern, you'd think she was a serial flinger but actually Joan didn't consider them flings – she saw them as short relationships that didn't work out. That of course sounded more romantic than flings!

When she met Michael, she despaired. He was great looking, funny, and intelligent. But – and it was a big but – he didn't seem to be a romantic. Early on, when she expected romantic gestures to start, there were no signs of them. Well at least she didn't consider it romantic when he sent a humorous card for her birthday the week after they met (others probably would that early on!). Instead thoughts like: 'He could've at least sent flowers or bought me a small gift – I would've done that for him,' ran through Joan's mind. 'And I had such high hopes!' Yes, and unreasonable ones, too!

In the past, Joan would've felt her efforts weren't appreciated. She'd then feel unworthy, get angry, and finish with the man. As it was so early on in the relationship and a friend urged Joan to 'get help' before she dumped what seemed like a nice guy, Joan went on her own for help. After exploring where her emotional neediness came from – and it *was* neediness being so romantically demanding – Joan was willing to put the brakes on her expectations.

##  Joan's Relationship Enhancement Strategies

Joan knew Michael was essentially the sort of man she was looking for. She was determined not to jeopardize their young relationship with her romantic expectations.

- ❤ Priorities – Joan made a relationship 'priority' list. She included those things she saw as lifelong qualities that a partner must have. Romance figured fairly high but Joan conceded that overall the qualities of caring personality, humour, intelligence, and taking responsibility were higher. She'd simply have to stick with things and coax the romance out of Michael.

- ❤ The positives – Joan was to focus on the positives Michael had to offer. Each day she was to remember his wonderful smile and his intelligent comments on recent events. She was also going to concentrate on her good points so she didn't feel so needy. Joan put 'reminders' around her flat of the good things she had. These self-affirmations were there to help remind her that she got her self-worth from things other than romance.

💜 Romantic possibilities – Joan made a list of the sorts of romantic gestures she'd like Michael to make. We arranged these from the most simple, 'I'd like him to compliment me,' (Yes, compliments are very romantic!) to the more complex, 'I'd love him to surprise me at work with a picnic lunch.' Joan thought of ways she could coax these from Michael with subtle hints.

💜 Romantic gestures – recognizing her 'too much, too soon' style that she was going to try and keep in check, she thought of how she might take a subtle approach to coaxing the romance out of Michael. She could, for example, compliment him without going over the top. She could take him to a romantic movie and afterwards discuss the movie. If Michael made any noises about the romantic element, she could encourage this even more. Joan could be affectionate to Michael (without going over-the-top in public! Something Joan had been accused of with her 'too much, too soon' style!), letting him know that she enjoyed displays of affection. As she got to know him more, she said she might drop little hints with romantic gestures. Joan suggested things like cooking him a candle-lit dinner with his favourite wine, or recording him a tape of his favourite music.

💜 Straight talking – within reasonable limits, there was no reason why Joan couldn't speak her mind, particularly if it came naturally into the conversation. For example, if they were talking about work, she could tell Michael that a romantic email would cheer her day up!

💜 Past experiences – then she listed romantic successes she'd experienced and thought about how orchestrated they'd been. Had she helped the men along in any way? If so, how had that worked? Had she completely led the way? Had it ever backfired? The answer was 'Yes' many had. Mulling over the past re-affirmed to her the need to slow down on her high expectations.

Joan felt more confident now that she'd thought things through rather than diving in head first. With her new attitude, she was going to try to encourage that elusive romance rather than demanding it and bailing out quickly if it didn't materialize. Joan came to realize that over-emphasizing romance in the past had put her relationships on a false footing. She was expecting men to meet unrealistic standards (at least the majority of men couldn't reach those!). It didn't mean in any way that she was compromising her relationship standards – Michael easily met those.

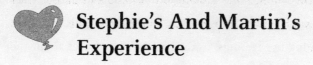

# Stephie's And Martin's Experience

Stephie's relationship style was quite the opposite of Joan's. Stephie had always given 'too little, too late' in her hopes of finding the perfect man. She longed for someone who would make a fuss of her, make her feel special, surprise her, and cherish her. At 27, she assumed she would already be in a solid relationship. Stephie always intended that once she found this man, she'd give him the same romantic love in return. So she'd meet someone new, bide her time, watch out for romantic signs, but never give of herself. Most of the men she dated got fed up with her apparent lack of interest. Little did they know she was desperately controlling showing her emotions in the hopes they'd give her some 'signs' first.

As Stephie was so hung up on romantic 'signs', she'd ignore the other things men did to show their interest. Like telephone when they said they would, go out on dates in a variety of settings, and generally try to relax and enjoy themselves.

Stephie had been dating Martin for about six months when she realized things were stuck. Martin was a very sweet guy who made the occasional rather clumsy romantic gesture. Clumsy because he wasn't sure just how much Stephie actually liked him. So, for example, he arranged to cook her favourite meal at his house. He was so wracked with nerves that he was all fingers and thumbs. Dinner was more chaos than canoodling! Stephie didn't do much to salvage the situation. Withholding her feelings as always, she teased him about the date disaster. When of course he'd rather have had loads of reassurance that it was the gesture that counted.

Inside she knew Martin was trying, so she decided it was time to take a different approach! It was dawning on Martin, now that Stephie was willing to be more honest, that if he hung in there they might work it out.

##  Stephie's And Martin's Relationship Enhancement Strategies

As it was still relatively early days in their relationship, a softly, softly approach was needed. They were both 'into' the relationship but weren't showing all their cards yet – especially considering Stephie's style.

- Changing her style – where had this 'too little, too late' style come from? When Stephie discussed her childhood, it was apparent her mother used to withhold love and only dish it out as a reward. It was a very conditional love. Stephie was actually doing the same. She'd dish out a little affection or attention when men made obvious gestures. But seeing as men usually need a great big sign saying, 'I like you!' to encourage them, Stephie had never got very far. Everyday she needed to remind herself that 'it feels good to get love so you've got to give a little too'. This became her mantra and Martin was sure to benefit.

💜 Romantic confidence – Martin needed to believe that he could be a romantic. Whatever gave him a warm feeling inside, he needed to try more of. So, for example, since he loved Stephie's wonderful smile he needed to tell her. And make it sound good! Practise makes perfect and perfect = confidence!

💜 Creative romance – Martin and Stephie needed to be honest about what made them feel warm and deliciously wonderful. But they were to have fun with it. Each was to plan a wonderful day out full of little surprises. And none of the surprises could involve buying presents – that's where the creativity came in! In their own time, both brainstormed little special pleasures for the other that they could string together into an entire day. The sorts of things included were Martin remembering how Stephie had once said she'd never seen a sunset over the ocean (while they were watching a documentary about ocean life). He planned the day he was responsible for at the seaside ending with them wrapped up warm together watching the sunset.

Stephie and Martin felt much more relaxed together. Stephie was getting a bit of the magic she wanted, and Martin was finding her 'too little, too late' barriers dropping. Romance is an important piece of the relationship puzzle that needs putting in perspective. We're often guilty of expecting romance from men who a) aren't naturally romantic, and b) are concerned with not appearing to undermine the way we feel. This comes back to the issue of modern men's confusion – what do women really want? So if your romantic piece of the puzzle is a huge one, and his is a small one, they may fit together in the end with the right approach.

We want to encourage romance because the right relationship with some wonderful romance mixed in can become the ultimate relationship! If you have a great guy who just doesn't seem that romantic, give him a chance – you may be able to coax it out of him!

 ## Some Key Messages To Remember About Men And Romance!

Romantic difference – romance is something men feel they '*have* to do' and women feel they '*want* to do'!

Men are not natural romantics – all these years they've been covering up their emotions. Being romantic is like them putting on a big sign saying, 'These are my emotions – take them!' – bear this in mind when you're getting to know him. And recognize what he thinks is romantic may be very different from what you think is. Mending your leaky pipe may be his grand gesture of love!

🗝 Romantic expectations – if you have high romantic expectations, either find your very own 'Valentino' or 'Don Juan', or put it in balance with the other qualities you feel are important. Then be positive about encouraging it.

🗝 Don't demand – if you demand romance, think again. Better to slowly coax it out of men than to push them so hard they resent you – not very romantic!

🗝 Encourage all their attempts! This will make them feel good and less vulnerable if you're loving and positive, and not teasing in any way.

🗝 Appreciate the word 'surprise'. When men use this word as in, 'I've got a surprise for you,' they usually think they're being romantic. Appreciate their surprise even if it's not what you had in mind. Like when they surprise you with a new mouse pad for your computer, but what you really wanted was that gorgeous new perfume you saw. Analyse the thought behind it. He thinks you'll be seeing your mouse pad all the time and thinking of him! At least he's trying and I'm sure as you develop your romantic intelligence, you'll coax more appropriate surprises out of him.

🔑 Praise them! Men are usually quite good once they've been praised for their attempts at romance! Even if he mucks up the dinner he's cooking for you, like Martin, tell him you love it.

🔑 Cooking up romance is *not* about playing games. You can hint, you can even ask for it but it's *not* about playing with a man's emotions. They'll close up like a clam and never get down to the important business of romance!

🔑 Lead by example! Show them that romance to you does not mean they have to keep you in fresh red roses (although I wouldn't say, 'No!'). Men invariably think it means spending money but that's not the case – show them how romantic you can be without dipping into your pocketbook. Give him a private pet name, record him some of his favourite songs, even the simple compliment can be romantic given in the right way!

🔑 Have fun! Most of all romance is about intimate fun. This is what will set your relationship apart. Enjoy it – don't make it a battleground. And you will get to the heart of your relationship potential.

Chapter Thirteen

# Understanding Men And Commitment

We've come to that all important word – the 'C' word – commitment! It's a natural progression after falling in love and wanting to spend more time with someone to start thinking in terms of what the relationship means. Is it serious? Is it monogamous? And how committed are you both to making it a happy, lasting relationship? Right from the start, women will discuss every detail of their new relationship with friends and/or family. They catalogue the events and emotions that signal a developing commitment. They may fear commitment, they may be confused about their feelings but they will still acknowledge something is happening. Even if, for example, they have a 'too little, too late' relationship style. It is a very rare woman who doesn't at least think through, and pre-plan the possibilities.

For men on the other hand, it's different. It's easy for confusion to arise when you think about the last few chapters. As you will now be aware (and were undoubtedly aware of it in the past but hadn't put your finger on it!) men think differently and so they will analyse how committed they are in a different way. Men feel differently and so the emotions they experience in a developing relationship will not mirror ours. And as they view sex and romance in a different way than we do this will also influence their view of commitment. To the romantic novice this makes predicting a man's level of commitment a difficult state of affairs to judge. Not that all women want commitment. Many are very happy to live an independent life dipping in and out of the dating scene. But for those who want commitment now or in the future hopefully this chapter will help you understand this important piece of the relationship puzzle.

# Do Men Look At Commitment In Their Straightforward Way?

Commitment for men is a minefield. Even though they tend to 'cut to the chase' in their daily life – in the way they think and feel with commitment they often behave in the opposite manner. This is where they lose their ability to be straightforward! They throw their hands up as if they're trying to ward off some evil curse. 'Commitment? What commitment? Not me. Not yet!' they protest. Unless of course they're the exception to the romantic rule. And there are always exceptions! Those rare men who say, 'Yes, I'm looking for someone to share my life with!' They're usually about 40 and have tried all other routes. They end up with the honesty route – much more of a female thing!

But let's get down to basics – why do they not look at commitment in the straightforward way they handle most things? Because men go into a type of emotional 'denial' when it comes to commitment. If they think about commitment they have to think about the *meaning* of their relationship. Something that doesn't come that naturally to lots of men. They've been dating someone for six months. Things are going well and they've dumped the other woman they'd been seeing months before realizing that one woman is enough. So things are straightforward – why go messing with what the meaning is?

As soon as we start making noises about our relationship with things like, 'How much do you care about me?' or, 'Am I the only person you're seeing?' they have to start giving the meaning of it all some thought. 'She's got something, there!' they think. 'Am I really involved?' they ask. 'It this it?', 'Will I never be with another woman?' These set off a chain reaction most men aren't used to which is why they feel so uncomfortable with it. Their 'cut-to-the-chase' attitude won't quite cut it when the hot topic of commitment finally lands in their lap!

 ## Do Men Really Feel Differently About Commitment?

Many women wonder if deep down men really do feel differently about commitment. They reason that even if men are frequently slower to disclose their true feelings that they're probably there somewhere. Yes, their feelings are there and yes, again they are different from ours! We could look at our ancient ancestors for part of the answer. Commitment to a family unit back in the times of the hunter-gatherer meant taking on responsibility for the woman's and subsequent offspring's welfare. Not only did the man have to do their own hunting and gathering and contribute to the community, this meant they had to take on and meet very real demands of additional work.

The relationship was mainly practical as far as they were concerned – they still got out and did the hunting and gathering. For women the nurturing role we've already discussed cast a different light on a long-term relationship. It was in their interest to keep things running smoothly so the man in their life kept providing. Of course now we don't need men to provide for us! But that familiar echo from the past still lurks in our genes. And it's hard to shake off. Combine this with the fairy tale and cinematic 'happy-ever-after' emotional diet we've been fed since childhood and the pull is strong to get our man and keep him. I'd like to think that nowadays women are doing this from a position of strength. That they want a relationship. That they want to share their life. But they make *their* choices about how it should happen!

And this is probably where the 'battle of the sexes' arose from – this tension about commitment. Men believing, or at least playing a part, that somehow it's something they have to *give in* to. That they are giving up some hard to define 'freedom' that supposedly we haven't experienced. In modern relationships, it shouldn't be about giving up freedom but gaining complementary experience and points of view that can extend us and enrich our lives.

# Where Do Difficulties Arise From Now?

Difficulties arise because many men do feel threatened by the 'C' word. They fear that once they give in to this, they will become vulnerable. Men imbue women with almost a mystical power that somehow we will control things once they start putting their cards on the table. And those cards include thinking about what the relationship means and expressing this.

Commitment to men is like erecting a big sign saying, 'Beware – loss of freedom and vulnerability pending!' Whereas for women it's more likely to be an exciting signpost to a deeper intimacy. Their internal sign says, 'Yes, I have found my soul mate!' Seeing as we come to commitment from these different ends of the spectrum you can see where difficulties arise. Successful negotiation of this stage of a relationship involves understanding this. You're all excited about getting close and they're all wary about how this is going to affect them.

 # What They Fear Most

What men fear most and what they actually end up enjoying is the emotional intimacy. Consider this: all your life you've been worried about a situation and you've built up all sorts of fears and internalized myths about it. Then when it actually happens you find out it's not so horrible after all. It's actually quite a pleasant state of affairs. With that huge release of tension, a great deal of satisfaction occurs. So men have built up all sorts of myths about what commitment will actually be like and then when they finally allow it to happen, they find it's not so bad after all. In fact it's quite a nice place to be! Understanding this will help you reach your relationship potential.

This doesn't mean you can announce to the man you want to commit to that, 'Oh, this isn't going to hurt so relax' – like some romantic dentist! No, you have to be aware of all that I'm saying and understand their point of view coming to that place. Their point of view (their fear and anxiety) is going to change but it will change successfully if it's not rushed, pressured, or pushed. There are some cases where ultimatums *have* to be issued. For example, you've been together for three years, you love him, and want to plan a family. He starts playing about emotionally and won't commit to you and the idea of having a family. At this point you have to decide whether he's worth hanging in for, or whether he's a no-hoper who does not share your future expectations of a committed relationship with children to boot!

# When Men Finally Fall

When men finally fall – they fall hard. And it's not just because of the enjoyment they suddenly get when they find that a committed relationship with the 'lovely you' isn't like their worst fears. No, it's more than that. Because once they've chosen to commit – and it's been a big deal – they do *not* want to go there again very quickly. All that build-up. All that vulnerability. No way! They've invested too much at this point so turning back is hard. Which is why most divorces are sought by women. We can actually move on from a situation that's unsatisfactory more easily than they can. Most men will admit that even if things aren't right, it's a lot more worrying to face being out there in that single world again than to coast along in the relationship. That very attitude is probably also why lots of women accuse their partners of being 'lazy' when it comes to the relationship.

Think of this as the 'battle of the sexes'. Like a battle, once they fall to the enemy, they are captured for good! There may be some plotting to escape, there may be some grumbling among the prisoners. But that's soon sorted out as they adjust to life after the battle under the new regime – yours!

# The Commitment Threshold

This relates to what I call the 'commitment threshold'. Everyone has one. It's that point when we cross into serious relationship territory. With men, it's a slow process of you totting up points in their eyes. Once the right amount of points has been reached, you've reached their commitment threshold and it's crossed.

Women tend to go through a relationship 'checklist' early on. We check off the qualities we want compared to what the new man in our life seems to have. Whereas men go through their own 'checklist' much later down the line. When they start to feel comfortable with you. When you start to feel comfortable with their friends. When you two have proven you can have fun in bed, etc. All these things slowly tot up in their mind and then you hit a magic number and bingo! You've made it over the threshold. Once you've managed to get them over their commitment threshold, then they'll want to stay put!

# How You Can Tell When They're Getting Involved And May Be Ready To Commit

So let's say you get to the stage where you know you're involved and interested in commitment. How can you tell if he's ready, willing, and able? There are three main ways to tell if your man is getting ready to commit. The first two are 'verbal' methods – what he 'says'. The third one is 'behavioural' – what he 'does'. Obviously the possible conversations you may have with him, and his behaviour, are infinite so I've chosen some straightforward examples to illustrate these:

1. He stops putting up hurdles and barriers to *your* more intimate conversations. You know what it's like when you're first dating. As soon as you get on personal territory his conversation dries up. For example, you go out with his friends one evening. At the end of the evening you remark that his best friend, Tom, seems 'insecure'. He simply shrugs it off and says, 'I don't think so.' As your relationship develops, if he's getting involved, he'll actually start responding to your more personal conversation. In Tom's case, he might say, 'Yeah, he's been hurt a lot and is wary around women.' That sort of verbal openness is a very positive sign to work with!

**2** He starts telling you more intimate things about his friends, family, issues at work, etc. When he starts initiating conversation about things more personal to him, you know he's getting comfortable with involvement. For example, at the beginning he may say things about work like, 'It's fine.' But when he starts saying things like, 'Things with my boss really got on top of me today,' or, 'I don't know how I'm going to handle the situation with my assistant,' you know he trusts you to be interested and care. Another positive sign!

**3** He lets his dating mask slip. He starts to show you the real him – warts and all – and hopes you like it! You will notice when his behaviour starts to relax. And when it feels and looks comfortable, then this is the last major sign he's involved. At the beginning you'd drop over to his house and he'd hurriedly tidy up the mess on the coffee table and ensure you had a place to put down your coffee cup. Now, though, when you arrive, he simply plops down on the sofa next to you, gives you a hug, and seems oblivious to the days-old cups and plates on the coffee table. You may take this as a sign he's taking *you* for granted. Actually it's the opposite in his book – it shows he feels comfortable enough around you to be himself! Knowledge of these three points will help you reach your relationship potential.

# Ways They're Likely To Try To Avoid Commitment

Men speak a lot of 'double talk' when the conversation turns to things like where the relationship is going and how committed they are to you. Take a look at some typical things men say along these lines and what they mean.

| The excuses you'll hear | What he means |
| --- | --- |
| 'I'm enjoying being single right now.' | 'You're not special enough to give up my freedom for!' |
| 'I've had bad experiences in the past.' | 'My feelings aren't strong enough to move on with you.' |
| 'Let's see how things progress.' | 'I'm not sure of my feelings.' |
| 'I don't think I'm right for you.' | 'You're not right for *me*!' |
| 'Let's just take things one step at a time.' | 'I'm in *no* hurry to get involved.' |
| 'I don't think I'm what you're looking for.' | 'You're not what I'm looking for.' |

When you hear these phrases, beware if you're getting involved! Either he's just not as interested (then don't waste your precious time!) or he's got huge barriers up. You have to ask yourself if he's worth breaking down barriers for.

Otherwise if he's fun then enjoy his company for some simple dating realizing it's unlikely to go anywhere.

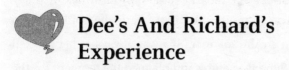

# Dee's And Richard's Experience

Dee had been slipping into a relationship with Richard for about six months. I say 'slipping' because Dee had a true 'It just happened!' (IJH) relationship style. Up until that point, she was not that bothered about how serious things got. Richard had quite a chequered past and had been in the death throws of a relationship when he took up with Dee. Now though, she was pregnant! Suddenly Richard's level of commitment became an issue. What were his feelings about the relationship? Was he committed? Pregnancy was like a great big wake-up call and Dee realized she wanted to commit.

Dee needed to be open and honest. With a baby on the way, there was no time for the usual 'gentle' strategies to determine Richard's intentions. At the same time Dee could not simply 'storm in' at an emotional level demanding to know what was going to happen. Particularly when she, herself, had been 'guilty' of IJH.

# 💜 Dee's Relationship Enhancement Strategies

Dee sought individual help. How could she handle this situation without Richard 'running a mile' to use her words?

💜 Honesty without pressure – people are frightened of honesty – they equate it with pressure but it's not. Dee needed to create an intimate moment where she could talk to Richard in a calm manner. She was always at her relaxed best on a Sunday evening and planned the moment for the coming Sunday over a quiet dinner.

💜 Verbal tactics – 1. Dee decided to ask him, without creating a drama, what he 'thought' about the impending arrival of the baby. Choosing your words carefully helps set the appropriate unpressured tone. Asking about a man's 'feelings' is more likely to raise their defences than asking about their 'thoughts'. 2. Dee was also going to be careful not to express her own thoughts in overly emotional ways. She'd definitely get farther with Richard this way. 3. Dee was aware of the value of using 'I statements' – beginning sentences with 'I think,' and 'I would like,' etc. This gives him a sense of her confidence through this verbal technique. His confidence may be raised by hers. Just as, if she presented herself as nerve-wracked, it may transfer to him too! Not helpful!

💜 Behavioural tactics – Dee was not going to crowd Richard with loads of affection. She'd always been the more demonstrative of the two and wanted to avoid any pressure that might put him on his guard.

💜 Enhancing commitment – Dee was going to present all the positives of their situation. As she had been relating in her IJH style, which she acknowledged, and Richard had rather slipped into things too, they'd never really talked about the good things they shared. It was time to enhance their future by acknowledging their positive present.

Sometimes checking your own expectations about how deep your relationship is becoming (and making sure they're grounded in reality!) and communicating clearly, as Dee learned to do, will help to sort out a commitment issue. However, it's not always that easy. The commitment issue comes into play at a greater or lesser extent depending on your relationship pattern and style. Obviously a 'too much, too soon' style may lead to insurmountable problems. If you have expectations that he'll be committed as quickly as you, within this style, you may actually frighten him off.

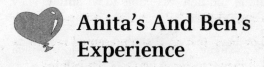

# Anita's And Ben's Experience

Anita's and Ben's experience illustrates this point about styles. Anita sought to recreate her parents' very devoted relationship. She had always looked for men that seemed able to fit into this expectation without much success though. Anita had tried to squash them into a relationship that suited her quite intense emotional needs. Instead of recognizing them for their unique qualities and how these might complement her as a person!

Anita was crazy about Ben who actually seemed to be the serious, thoughtful type (like her adored father) but who had not mentioned the 'C' word. Anita's patience had worn thin and she'd started to push Ben on this issue. Now what once seemed like the perfect relationship was heading for troubled waters. Ben was digging his feet in. Although he enjoyed what they had and loved Anita, he didn't like the feeling of pressure.

## 💗 Anita's And Ben's Relationship Enhancement Strategies

Anita and Ben decided to sort out their differences.

💗 Exploration – both agreed they needed to explore their thoughts and feelings in a contained environment. Otherwise Anita, with her fiery temperament was liable to fly off the handle, and Ben was liable to withdraw. They explored the good things they shared, which were actually quite a few. They explored their future expectations, which weren't terribly mismatched. And they explored how they could compromise. One solution was to try living together with a view to deciding in six months whether or not they would commit. This way Ben didn't feel pressured and Anita felt it wasn't an indefinite wait.

- ❤ Expressing need – both needed to learn to express their emotional needs in the most positive way. Emotional need often dictates behaviour in relation to gaining a commitment. If you are needy, you behave in a needy way in order to gain the attention and commitment you're seeking. Anita needed to try some calming strategies to keep her rather boisterous approach to emotions in check. And Ben needed to learn that having come this far he could start verbalizing more of his needs. He certainly demonstrated physical commitment with lots of affection and a relaxed manner around Anita. This needed to transfer to his conversation.

- ❤ Mutual ground – this can involve the actual physical environment – like how comfortable you feel discussing things on your own territory compared to your boyfriend's. It can also include an emotional ground. Where you've come to in your conversations and how safe you feel on different topic areas. Ben had always felt threatened when things got too emotional at Dee's place because he felt surrounded by her family. Dee's home was similar to her parents' in feel, and it had a very strong stamp on it. It's incredible how such considerations can affect the progress of conversations. They agreed that until Ben moved in, which they were planning, mutually comfortable ground should be chosen for discussions. Once Ben moved in, they planned how his things could fit in with Anita's – so he wouldn't always feel like a guest!

♥ Compromise – so that things could progress without pressure, they agreed a compromise. Anita was not to mention her parents' relationship (which she was very proud of and frequently used as a point of comparison) or bring up their six month deadline. Ben was to keep the process of opening up communication going.

As you can see the subject of 'men and commitment' is not straightforward. They usually feel differently about it and approach it in a different way. This can be successfully negotiated! You may not be ready or want to commit – that's great. But for those who do, this is a major piece of the relationship puzzle to get to grips with. To feel part of a committed, loving relationship is a wonderful experience and one that enhances us as human beings. It's about sharing, compromise, and enjoying true emotional and sexual intimacy. Reaching that level of human companionship is about two people complementing each other's nature and forming a strong bond with which to face life. You can reach your relationship potential if you balance your feelings about commitment with the way he's likely to approach it.

# Some Key Messages To Remember About Men And Commitment

**Men are capable of commitment!** Just because they look at commitment and what it means differently, their way is every bit as valid as yours.

**Their thinking will catch up with yours!** You may, early on, tick off their long-term potential and qualities. They simply do this later on. We use emotional evidence and intuition. They slowly build a case: 'Yes she does get on with my friends.' 'Yes, she does enjoy the same leisure pursuits.' 'Yes I do feel comfortable with her.' Etc.!

**Commitment makes them vulnerable!** Remember, we tend to see commitment as a strengthening experience. They tend to see it as an experience that leads to vulnerability.

**Coax commitment gently!** Coax them up to their commitment threshold. Making casual remarks at the appropriate time and spaced as necessary will do it. One week you might mention, 'We do get on in bed, don't we?' You've planted that fact. A couple of weeks later you might add, 'I like your friends.' Etc. As you build the case for them to see that things are going nicely, so they'll get nearer to commitment. And they'll feel as if they're mutually in control.

🗝 Don't confuse it with a game! Commitment is not a competition to see who can beat the other! If you start playing emotional games at this stage of your relationship, they're more than likely to backfire.

🗝 Once they've fallen, watch out for the three main signs that they're getting involved and on the road to commitment. They start to respond to your verbal exploration. Their own verbal exploration gets more intimate. They drop their dating mask showing you their warts and all.

🗝 You can work out the non-committal types! Beware of the phrases they use when you sound them out about the state of your blossoming relationship. Study the table in this chapter.

🗝 Watch out! Men who want to womanize will play on your commitment buttons. If you sense they're not being genuine as they snowball you with loads of, 'I can't believe how quickly I'm falling in love,' etc., then don't believe it! Keep an eye on whether their behaviour matches their words.

Chapter Fourteen

# You & Him

Conclusions!

This is the exciting part! It's time to string together all you've learned about the relationship puzzle. This will ensure you get to the heart of your relationship potential – and we all have so much untapped potential. It just takes more understanding. *You & Him* is about understanding *you*, and all the pieces that go to making you the unique person you bring to relationships. And it's about understanding *him* – how he thinks, feels, and his attitudes towards sex, romance, and commitment. These combine to make the unique person he brings to relationships.

Understanding both of you will enhance the way you and him fit together – like two comfortable, loving puzzle pieces.

 ## Putting Together The Pieces Of Your Relationship Puzzle

When entering into romantic relationships and maximizing your true potential, you need to think of it as a series of pieces. You may battle at times, as certain pieces don't seem to fit. At other times things seem to click into place straightaway – the pieces interlock nicely. Most of the time things fall somewhere in between – they need a little bit of jigging around (understanding!) to slide into place.

 ## The Two Big Romantic Mistakes You *Can* Avoid

The big mistake many women make is trying to find a puzzle piece the *same* as theirs! Would that work? No! Puzzle pieces have to have complementary shapes that fit together neatly into a complete form. You could search forever for a man 'like you' but it's unlikely you'll find one. 'Why can't he be more like me?' I hear constantly. As you've now seen, men don't think, feel, or approach relationships in the same way so enjoy them for who they are. You know the saying: 'Two heads are better than one.' But they wouldn't be if they were the same!

The next big mistake women make is to try to squash a man into fitting in with their puzzle piece. You've developed enough romantic sense to realize you won't find a man like you, but then you go on to try to change the men you meet! Yes, you try to change him so that he's more like your father, or like some ideal you've got in mind. Usually based on a romantic checklist you've dreamed up over the years.

Men have their own individual background and view of life. How would you feel if a man were trying to change you? Not very good, I'm sure. And quite understandably, they'd rather be accepted for who they are, than feel as if you're moulding them like some romantic experiment (of course you *should* expect certain basic human qualities like respect and kindness). But with compromise, over time, you'll adapt to each other's needs. This will help you grow in your potential to have healthy relationships.

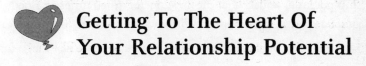

# Getting To The Heart Of Your Relationship Potential

Think how complex you are! There are all sorts of things you have going on with your inner romantic dialogue. Right from when you first meet a new man, through the first few dates, and beyond, your mind works constantly. It mulls over those delicious first feelings of interest. It then passes over your relationship track record – weighing up how much he might be like, or different from, your last partner. Next it fast-forwards to that great romantic unknown – the future.

Now I hope you're armed with enough romantic knowledge for your inner dialogue to work for you rather than against! We can all enjoy wonderful, romantic relationships. You *can* stop making typical relationship mistakes. I'm sure you've identified your relationship pattern and won't stay locked into one that doesn't suit your needs at the moment. And now you've recognized and thought about your relationship style, you don't have to be a Goldilocks compelled to relate in a style that hasn't worked for you! I hope you have a better understanding of the way he thinks, feels, and approaches sex, romance, and commitment. After a few romantic experiences, you don't have to feel you've entered an episode of *The X Files*. Now you can see how he might truly complement you. This understanding will help you reach the heart of your relationship potential – just what the 'love doctor' (me!) ordered. Good luck – *you* deserve it!

# The 'F Factor' Quiz

Over the years, I've come to the conclusion that my five 'F factors' can determine the quality of your relationships and whether or not they'll last. If you're in a relationship, or when you meet someone new, consider the 'F factors'! These five 'F factors' are 'family background', 'friendship circle', 'fanciability', 'financial agreement' and 'fun'. They represent the likely areas to cause problems for you, or help you reach your relationship potential.

The 'F factors' cover the main areas of our lives. And if you want to share your life with someone, it's best to be compatible on most of these. Opposites do attract but usually only until they get bored with each other! Lasting love is usually based on mutual attitudes and interests covering family, finances, fun, friends, and how much you fancy each other!

# Do You Two Have The 'F Factors' In Your Relationship?

Select your most likely answer and then read the guidelines to find out.

## Factor One – Family Background

1. Do your families have similar income levels and attitudes to life? Yes/No

2. When you met did you feel you'd known each other all your lives? Yes/No

3. Do you feel at home with each other's families?  Yes/No

4. Do you have similar numbers of brothers and sisters? Yes/No

5. Are you on equally good terms with each other's families? Yes/No

## Factor Two – Friendship Circle

1. Do you like each other's friends?  Yes/No

2. Do you take turns seeing each other's friends?  Yes/No

3. Do you strike a good balance between seeing friends and spending time on your own?  Yes/No

4. Do you have similar attitudes to the importance of friend-ships?  Yes/No

5. Did you share some of the same friends before you were involved?  Yes/No

## Factor Three – Fanciability

1. Would you two agree that you make love frequently enough? Yes/No

2. Can you talk to each other about your sexual needs? Yes/No

3. Are you two as affectionate as you would like to be? Yes/No

4. Do you have similar attitudes to how important looks are? Yes/No

5. Do you place equal importance on romance? Yes/No

## Factor Four – Financial Agreement

1. Do you think you'd make major financial decisions together? Yes/No

2. Would it be unlikely for either of you to accuse the other of overspending? Yes/No

3. Do you share the same 'life plan' in terms of investments, savings, and moving up the property ladder? Yes/No

4. Would you easily agree on how to spend a windfall? Yes/No

5. Would you spend roughly the same amount on presents? Yes/No

## Factor Five – Fun Factor

❤ 1   Do you like the same sorts of music, movies, and books? Yes/No

❤ 2   If you suddenly had a free day, would you easily agree what to do? Yes/No

❤ 3   Do you two put the same importance on leisure time? Yes/No

❤ 4   Would you be unlikely to argue about what to watch on television? Yes/No

❤ 5   Would it be easy to agree where to go on holiday? Yes/No

Look at each 'F factor' individually. Five 'Yes' answers out of five, indicates you have great compatibility/harmony on this factor. Three or four 'Yes' answers means you have good compatibility/harmony on this factor. Two or less 'Yes' answers out of five means you need be aware of that factor. You are likely to run into trouble in this part of your relationship. The more factors you have 'great' or 'good' compatibility/harmony on, the greater the chance your relationship will thrive.

For each 'F factor' you have two or less 'Yes' answers, explore whether this causes you trouble or not. It may be that this one area actually doesn't affect your relationship much –

particularly if you have high levels of compatibility/harmony on the rest. For example, except for the 'friendship factor' you have high compatibility. But you've both come to an agreement that you don't really like each other's friends and so you socialize independently once or twice a week. Such a negotiated compromise can work! Alternatively this area could be causing you real problems. For example, one of you spends far more time with their friends than the other. You're going to need to work on this! Identifying these problem areas by separating out the 'F factors' can help you solve them.

If overall on three or more 'F factors' you do not have at least good compatibility your relationship is likely to run into trouble. If you're in the first mystery phase of passion, it may not seem important now. But as time goes on, the elements making up each 'F factor' take on more importance. Ask yourself why you are so attracted to this person. Could it be due to your style that's keeping you locked into a cycle of unhappy relationships? If this person has qualities you genuinely like, then now is the time to enhance your relationship potential by improving your compatibility on the vulnerable 'F factors'! Leaving it until the passion fizzles out may be too late.

If you hit problems later on down the line, you may still like to disentangle difficult and negative emotions by seeing if the problems fit into the 'F factors'. You may find that one area alone is jeopardizing the rest of the relationship. The 'F factors' can help give you this clarity.

In your future romantic relationships use the 'F factors' as a guide to the potential staying power you two have. These are a guide for life to help you get to the heart of your relationship potential!